# KUNLUI

*The Path of Inner Alchemy*
*Leading to the Truth Within*

## Max Christensen

Published by Primordial Alchemist, LLC.

For inquiries contact Primordial Alchemist:
info@primordialalchemist.com

Editing by Brothers Tao
and Compass Rose Horizons
Cover Design by Naya Rice
Japanese Translation of Foreword by Eika Cain
Photography by Kathleen Blacklock: www.kblacklockphotography.com
Subject Model Diana Aubrey

ISBN: 978-0-9852236-0-1

Printed in the United States of America

I would like to express my thanks to the spirit of the great mystery known as Tao for giving me the wonderful chance to live upon this beautiful world. I thank the world of spirit for granting me the unique experiences of meeting many great masters of various mystical traditions. I sincerely thank these great masters who have allowed me to express their life teachings through the spiritual system known to many throughout the world as the KUNLUN System. May these simple yet profound teachings give those searching for their spiritual roots the gifts to awaken their own spiritual perfection within themselves and help bring the world and all of life into a state of balance and harmony.

— Max Christensen

# Disclaimer

The information presented in this book is based on the author's personal experience and is presented for the purpose of education and empowerment of each person on the path of awakening his or her own divine potential. The techniques explained in this book are to be used with discretion and reader's liability. The author is not responsible or liable in any manner for any body sensations, experiences, and possible issues resulting from applying the techniques explained in this book. Results and success in these practices will be unique to every individual. The reader of this publication assumes all responsibility for the use of these materials and information, which is in no way intended as a substitute for any physical, mental, or emotional healthcare, nor does it replace consultation with a competent healthcare professional. The contents should not be considered as a form of therapy, advice, direction, diagnosis, or treatment of any kind. If expert advice or counseling is needed, services of a competent professional should be sought. The author is not responsible for misuse of any material contained within this book or injury resulting from improper usage of the information found within this book. Individuals who read this book are not granted authority to teach or represent the KUNLUN System. Only certified apprentices and facilitators are authorized to teach these practices.

# Table of Contents

# Foreword

My initial meeting with Max Christensen had a strong impact on me. In seeking the truth, I had visited so many masters of different traditions. Masters of the martial arts and shamans that I found all over the world would convey their ancient wisdoms to me. However, my first meeting with Max was so special that it made previous experiences suffused. I realized I had found a man who made good use of energy with an ease that seemed to be beyond time and space.

One month before our first meeting, I was on the island of Bali in Indonesia. I spent my days with a certain shaman who heals sickness in people and helps them by communicating with the spirits and also by manipulating the weather. He was a man of legend who cast spells over honey, creating a substance that would ignite his cigarette.

One day the man told me, "Kan, a special meeting will be coming to you soon. This man you will meet has succeeded in learning the true, ancient wisdoms. He is a rare person who holds the energy of the future. I can't hold a candle to his skills. I am glad to tell you this information, so please go back to Japan."

In 2005, I met Max in a small room of a certain building in Tokyo. I will never forget the moment my eyes met his. His mysterious blue eyes seemed to expand like the universe before me. They seemed to expand like the space in the universe and then twisted. I sensed through him the root of all things and that he was an expression of it. This is the living root of

KUNLUN System that Max told me about. Since that first meeting, time has passed. I am now living my miraculous life, and within my life there are no serious matters. I live my life by comfortably communicating with nature and the universe. I am traveling the world, teaching the KUNLUN System, which has connected me and Max together. I am continually meeting with people with whom I share this wonderful knowledge.

The path of KUNLUN System that Max teaches has led to incredibly fast changes. There is something powerful and unique that has to do with the fineness of the frequency. What makes this function, this awakening, possible? I should say it is from Max, who is a true master who has taken over these once-secret practices and succeeded at developing them. Only this person we know as Max took this knowledge and developed it correctly so that it can be used in the present day. Actually, when I had the transmission of the gold dragon body from Max, I met various (normally unseen) masters standing behind Max during that time of transmission. Max always says to me "Kan, it is up to you to wish for whatever you want to do in your life." Yes, I understood, and I had never been forced by Max to do anything I did not wish to do. Some masters only talk and make themselves sound good; some of them have very strong power. But many of these masters are driven by their own egos to control others. There are so many so-called masters like that.

Max jokes like a little boy, and the truth is that I have never heard of Max ever speaking ill of others. He also allows me to be his brother instead of his disciple. For Max, having power over others has no meaning. Whenever I see him, we tackle each other like children and we laugh. Some people have seen us doing this and said we looked like dogs playing with each other, and then they, too, laughed. I feel infinite energy here; I can't help feeling the real connection with the Tao. When my brother opens his heart to me, I feel the true master inside him.

Kan-san
Japan

# Preface

I have devoted my life to unraveling the great spiritual truths of the universe through my studies with various masters, past and present, and their chosen systems of awakening. I have sought to understand the underlying principle or root that all these systems have in common. After spending most of my life searching and studying, I eventually created a unique system of awakening, comprised of many of my teachers' accomplishments, along with my own discoveries. I call this system the KUNLUN System out of respect to not just one teacher, but to all of my past teachers, their arts, and achievements. The KUNLUN System is a system of practices offered for those seeking a spiritual path of internal alchemy leading to the truth within. There are various forms of Kunlun martial arts and Taoist qi-gung schools relating to the Kunlun Mountains, and each school has its own unique philosophies and tastes in training the body, mind, and spirit. To me, KUNLUN Name refers to the *mountain of the immortals*, the place of *no more learning,* and also the *root* leading to inner expression.

As you read this book, the art of the KUNLUN System has spread throughout the world, bringing happiness and blissful awakenings to places where spirituality is needed, by people devoted to helping both themselves and others who are less fortunate or living in inaccessible areas where there are no teachings or teachers. This book is a simple expression of my continued desire to help the world to become a better place for all beings and to bring awakening to all who seek the truth within themselves. I do not proclaim myself a master or a sifu, just a simple man who made a choice to help those seeking a spiritual path. It is my desire to simply reveal that the true elixir of awakening must come from both the energy of Tao and the merging of the childlike nature of one's own heart. The simple methods within this book will help you to begin to awaken yourself naturally, without force and without using your seeking mind, but through the action of the downward or water path system of *self-surrender*. This is the essence of Taoist Internal Alchemy.

# Chapter One

## *The Tao of Awakening and the Childlike Simplicity Approach*

Within the Taoist school of thought, there are many methods and ways to awaken one's self through body, mind, spirit, breath, form, or emptiness. I have had many masters tell me that emptiness was a way to awakening, to become without emotion, internal or external. I recognized that Alchemy was the proper means to awaken one's spiritual self, but after spending much time studying, I felt that there had to be a simpler way to become naturally awakened without being immersed in dogma. At the same time, I also discovered that we have access to so many ways but in reality have so little time. I found that listening and trusting in one's natural being in the moment, without attachment, along with true virtue and deep feeling, provides not only the key to nature itself, but also allows entrance to the truth hidden within ourselves; truth that became lost due to worldly distractions.

Perhaps the simplest yet most meaningful teaching that I always stress is the importance of maintaining a simple, childlike, playful nature. In addition to maintaining a childlike nature, positive virtues, and deep feeling, I also believe and teach the importance of embracing and refining your emotions, feeling nature both inside and out, and simply being in the moment where past, present, and future exist in the now. This mindset is a significant and fundamental aspect of the KUNLUN System.

Understanding nature and using the five elements of the mind and body to purify ourselves are also important foundational principles of the KUNLUN System. The process of purification allows us to eventually flow naturally into emptiness. By flowing with nature's five elements, the microcosm and macrocosm come into harmony and balance.

As we become adults, we often lose the root, childlike excitement of life and its mysteries. This is the unfortunate moment when we began to drift away from our true nature. What is the cause of this? When you were a newborn baby, you were pure, with the light still glowing in your eyes and heart. Then one day, someone comes along and sees something they don't like about you. These people pick on you until you either change their dislikes about you or you change yourself in order not to be picked upon.

As the years go by and this behavior becomes habitual, you may find yourself as only an image of other people's desires. You have lost yourself and now seek something more than what you see. Perhaps you become interested in spirituality, read many books, travel to other countries, but eventually you come home dismayed. You traveled on the path that was and is important but in vain, your heart still seeking the path of truth fulfilled in life. Then, when you give up the search, the right teaching comes along. But you had to travel outside yourself before discovering the truth that the path was inside the entire time. When you are no longer looking, the right path reveals itself. This is what I term *surrendering to the divine*.

So, now this KUNLUN System comes into your life. Is it by interest or accident? Understanding that everything and everyone has a purpose, you realize that there is more to life than growing up, working, growing old, and dying. You may ask yourself questions like "Why am I here?" or "What is the true purpose of my birth?" As you begin this simple approach to awakening, you will shake off what no longer serves you. Like water off a wet dog, you will shake off the gross stuff that holds you back, including whatever the people of your past have laid on you to make you forget your life's purpose. Just remember that for everything you let go of, you will be renewed and filled with the bliss, the elixir of life.

## What is Our Spiritual Purpose?

This question is frequently asked of me. Before the discussion goes any further, I ask: What is spirituality to you? Many people do not think about what form of spirituality they seek. For one person, it may be as simple as being one with nature, while another may choose to be a temple monk, while someone else has a different calling. Some people, in the moment, think that what they have found is what they want, but the truth of the matter is that if you know what you want as an outcome at the end of the path, then you can spend the necessary time to get to your destination instead of wandering around aimlessly, searching for a spiritual path.

When I recall the times I sought wisdom from my teachers from all the various traditions, the one thing that stands out most is the discovery that true enlightenment is the sense of total joy and freedom of the self, freedom from the suffering and attachments that hold us in the chains of inner darkness.

One of my teachers stressed the important union of the awakened heart with the powerful energies within the body.

Another taught that the union of bliss and emptiness was paramount. And yet another stressed the power of speaking the truth from the heart without ego or judgment. I have found that the heart is the gateway of truth and is capable of and responsible for balancing and refining the five emotions of our *monkey mind*, an important key to self-awakening.

One day my Taoist teacher asked me, "What is enlightenment to you?" My response included something to the effect of, "It is something, if true, that could only be laughed about, much like what the Tibetan tradition calls *crazy wisdom,* or entering the realm of the great mystery known as Tao." My teacher replied, "First you must become aware that there is a path to follow, then later you will become awake knowing that the path is within you, lastly an enlightened person would never say he or she is enlightened because the true Tao cannot be explained, only directly experienced from within or laughed about." I was also given a stern warning, which has proven to be a valuable lesson: "The wise man always walks with his head bowed in humbleness." I was then asked by my teacher to state the form of enlightenment I had been seeking. I replied that I wished to become illuminated from within, much like the Tibetan rainbow body, or as the Taoists call it, the indestructible diamond body. With this goal in mind, and with the cooperation and help of all my teachers through the years, I discovered my purpose and passion, and in time, the KUNLUN System was born.

I have been repeatedly asked to explain the concept of enlightenment. Well, from my perspective, what I have seen over and over again is that we first become aware that there is something missing in our life, something special and unseen. As we develop our inner sensitivity through various methods, we suddenly become aware that what we see and experience with the five senses is limited, but when a sixth sense starts to slowly develop, there is the awakening, a realization or illumination that we are light beings in a physical form, and at this level there is the emanation of light from deep within. It is a spiritual light seen only by sensitive people when their *sky eye* opens, not by people with limited openness. In various traditions throughout the world, this level of illumination is called the indestructible diamond body, the gold dragon body, the red phoenix of the nine palaces, *moksha*, and the returnable rainbow body — just to name a few reflections of this spiritual attainment. Enlightenment is the culmination of one's spiritual life on Earth, which can come to one's soul before death, during the dying process, or even after their life on Earth has finished. As to variations of such matters, there are different levels and forms of enlightenment, again based on the systems of awakening. The Taoist way of the diamond body, gold dragon, and red phoenix body are forms of practice leading to the great opening towards enlightenment.

# Chapter Two

## *Developing Proper Mindset and Breathing the One Breath*

I t is of great importance to develop the proper mindset when beginning your practice. I recommend allowing your linear, everyday mind to sink down into the expanse of the open heart, connecting the lower mind of the head with the higher spiritual mind within the heart. When the energy center called the middle dantien, or heart, connects with the upper dantien, or head, a union occurs, and the energetic channel called the katika channel, or channel of clarity, opens. Always remember to lead the mind of the upper dantien to the house of the heart, the middle dantien. In Tibetan spirituality, when this channel opens through the union of emptiness and bliss, awakening of the self unfolds. This is an extremely important aspect of the training. It is very important because as we open to our vastness from within, a blissful vapor, much like plasma, fills the katika channel and the heart space and is a sign that you are positively moving toward your goal.

Another important aspect is the energetic tension between the physical body and the energetic body. Take, for instance, the concept of a teeter-totter. When there is equal weight on each end, the teeter-totter is in balance, and there is no movement between each end unless force is applied to one end or the other. Now if we use the concept of creating an energy flow between the physical body and the energetic body, like a teeter-totter, a subtle nudge on the energetic body by using intentional methods of enlightenment will create a current of energy that will flow from one point to another or from the energetic body to the physical body. In this case, active kinetic energy is created instead of potential energy at rest. One simple way to create this nudge is, as you are sitting, imagine and feel as though you are standing up, and when you are standing, feel and imagine you are sitting down. This also applies when practicing lying down: imagine you are sitting upright. This creates the energetic tension for energy to flow.

I was once asked by one of my teachers if I understood the *One Breath*. I replied with what I thought, after many years of training, was the correct answer, and of course I got it wrong.

The *One Breath* is the merging of the inhale and the exhale through the nose, with the breath's physical movement located at the lower dantien, or in the lowest part of the abdomen. When you breathe in and out without a gap between these two cycles, the separation or polarity starts to gradually fall away. When there is a separation between the inhale and the exhale, this can be an early sign of one's health slowly failing. This gap of breath is caused by internal tension between the upper and lower body. Proper breathing occurs within the lower dantien, not the chest. This lower breathing will allow the movement of internal organs, massaging them through peaceful and unforced diaphragm breathing, continuing the flow of life into unity without the separation of the inhale to the exhale, the yin into the yang. This unity will create the formless form of Wu Chi.

The *One Breath* also helps to calm the mind, which affects the proper flow of blood and qi. Eventually, at the higher states of being, the outer breath and its obvious physical movements eventually become more and more subtle to the point that air movement is not really felt because the inner breath awakens. The Taoists call this skin breathing, since the skin acts as a second lung. To explain this concept, here is an illustration.

If you have ever jumped from an airplane, you would find yourself not breathing normally; this is from the air pressure forcing oxygen through the pores of your skin. Our methods produce the same phenomenon. Proper, relaxed breathing is vital to qi flow. The skin breathing prepares us for the mini-death of awakening, where gross bodily functions are changed into subtle energy absorbers of the quantum field. In addition, it addresses environmental factors that, although seemingly unrelated, affect our ability to effectively invite the universe to play with us. This partially addresses why energy or qi flow is affected by the breath, the weather, the mind, or other aspects of one's life at any moment in time.

If while doing the *One Breath* you experience many thoughts entering your mind, just let them flow without fixating or needing to act on them. Eventually, your mind will become still, and without the mind getting in the way or grasping onto thoughts, the *One Breath* will reveal deeper things to you.

During this breathing, if you focus your breathing on the lower dantien, it will become nice and warm. The middle dantien or heart region will become calm, and the upper dantien, the head, will become empty.

In alchemy, the lower dantien is like fire (Earth), the middle becomes like water (Human), and the upper dantien becomes the air (Heaven) element. Now that we have the proper mind set and breathing focus and are floating in a non-attached state, let us continue on our spiritual adventure.

# Positive Virtue: Its Effects on Body, Mind, and Spirit

Have you ever noticed the affect of positive or negative thinking and emotional states of being on your spiritual journey or outer life? Positive virtue is an essential focus in many different traditions of awakening. Before I get any further into this part of the journey, let me offer you two tips that I as well as many of my students have found very useful in times of hardship or when you are experiencing body or mind purification. The first thing I want to share with you is that it is always good to be non-attached to any OH-wows, just simply let them pass through you. Also, remember to SMILE. All Taoists know that this simple action of smiling is of great benefit and value. Smiling opens the energy at the top of the crown of the skull and lifts up the organs, freeing them of the heavy energy of standing or thinking. Smiling makes us feel better and can improve our outlook on life. Lastly, when we direct a smile towards another person, we light them up as we look at them, passing on the recognition of their beauty as a human being and the joy of meeting, if only for a second.

I also have a little secret, perhaps a brainteaser, which I share with my friends and wish to share with you: *Mind is Gravity*. If you take time to understand this concept, it will reveal important truths to you. As your mind affects the body directly, you should remember that the body is merely a reflection, a receptacle of the positive and negative experiences of the mind. An example of negative virtue is when the mind is focused on or disturbed by something upsetting, and the body feels dense or heavy. When you feel angry or depressed, what do you notice with your heart? Well, I have noticed that when I am happy or keeping in positive virtue, my heart feels light, and when negative virtues or upsetting feelings arise, my heart feels heavy. When I feel lighthearted, it is because my heart truly is light and free. Positive thoughts, feelings, and virtues allow the heart to float freely in neutral buoyancy within the pericardial sack, which surrounds and holds the heart, which in this state is free of physical gravity or gravity of the mind. The pericardial fluid surrounding the heart keeps the heart free of the push-pull of gravity on the organ itself. The blissful plasma-like vapor within the katika channel, discussed earlier in Chapter One, fills the pericardium, and the energetic charges created by such phenomenon cause the heart to float or defy gravity by virtue of the repelling charges that are created by the plasma charge against the myocardial charge. When I am heavy hearted, the heat of the energy of an agitated mind shrinks the pericardial sack around the heart, restricting the neutral buoyancy, giving the sensation of heaviness or tightness within the chest. Chronic stress, worry, or heaviness can create fibrous adhesions between the pericardial sac and the myocardium of the heart, restricting the heart motion. The blissful vapor or plasma field is gone and the heart is left struggling against its own prison, the pericardial sac. This will directly affect breathing, proper diaphragm movement, the brain, and the digestive function of the esophagus and stomach. Symptoms including shortness of breath, anxiety, angina, attention deficit disorder, heartburn, malabsorption, gastritis, or bloating can all occur and cause us to feel ill and out of sorts.

So, my friend, you can see how your mind has a direct influence on the physical workings of the human body. Virtue and emotions go hand in hand. When we focus on negative emotions, we tend to become non-virtuous in our daily actions. Wanting for power over others, allowing one's ego to get out of control, thinking one is better than others, and not caring about how we may affect others around us are all common occurrences when our negative emotions get the upper hand. When a person acts in this manner, his or her level of spiritual attainment will become rather limited. Oftentimes this leads to spiritual envy of those who humbly practice and maintain positive virtues. It is not uncommon that these types of people also have the habit of insulting others or making others on the path feel bad or inferior. This kind of behavior often gives the person who is perpetrating the negative virtues a sense of satisfaction, albeit negative satisfaction.

You see, the world is full of this kind of habitual programming, and yes, it takes real and honest effort to change one's self and one's view of the world. It requires taking constant inventory and self-observation, but with time, we can change these habits by simply practicing proper living, respecting others, being in and honoring nature, and simply *walking the royal path humbly.* Living by example and deed in positive virtue, as the ancient teachers did, cannot be overstressed and will insure that your path to Spirit will become less of a struggle.

Focusing on the feminine energy of your heart, living in harmony with the universe and nature, and simply treating others as you would like to be treated is, in my opinion, the most important philosophy to follow while on your path. It is not required to sacrifice yourself to cure others or to give, give, give until exhausted. My sifu once said when we do the work from within ourselves, the microcosm or universe inside becomes lit up, and this energy has a profound effect on the macrocosm, the outer universe, since they are both connected. Another view of the same understanding is revealed by one of my favorite quotes by a Tibetan yogi called Milarepa, who is remembered for stating, "When I am alone in the cave, I am connected with all things outside of myself." My teachers also said to me that "the blind cannot lead the blind," meaning if you have not mastered your own art both inside and outside yourself, how can you help others without having repercussions to the both of you?

Positive virtue vs. negative virtue is something many people never think about during the journey of self-awakening. Focusing on positive virtue leads to a greater opening and depth of experience of the path, while negative virtue closes the doors to greater understanding of the self and the Tao. Yes, the choice is yours to decide, so ponder deeply your journey within this short life, and please, choose well.

## Understanding and Embracing the Feminine Energy

Let us speak about the subject of embracing the feminine energy with regard to awakening and the KUNLUN System. In many spiritual traditions, embracing the universal female energy was considered a highly important piece of the puzzle, so to say. In my understanding and from experiences with female teachers, I have found that if one embraces one's spiritual path with an inner female-like essence, embracing one's own inner compassion and positive emotions of love, joy, happiness, and well-being, and joyfully lives one's art of awakening, he or she will discover how this way of being changes the energetic structure of one's mind, body, and spirit, opening the door to self-illumination.

In addition, all great masters who attained the highest spiritual levels laughed a lot because they realized the simplicity of being. This understanding was called *crazy wisdom*, and when they attained their exalted states of blissful awareness, these masters understood the importance of uniting the male and female energies or inner congress within their own bodies, through the energy channels called the sun, moon, and central channels of the energy body. When these channels of energy merge in harmony, the central channel, also known as the thrusting channel, activates and, in a sense, gives birth to the higher self through this channel.

As we continue to do the practices we have learned on our path, an energy channel eventually opens from the *crystal palace* in the brain center, which then unites with the great radiant pearl, Ben-Ben stone, or wish-fulfilling gem within the heart. This channel, carrying the blissful plasma or light vapor, is known in Tibetan yoga as the katika channel or the channel of clarity. When the mundane mind has attained stillness within the head, the adept allows the empty mind of the formless form to descend down through the katika channel to merge with the divine feminine essence of the heart, the universe within, or the higher mind (heart) of self. This is the union of form and non-form, of bliss and emptiness that interpenetrate one another. In this mystical union, when the perfected emotions of bliss and emptiness merge with the energy of the universe inside the heart, one feels a magnetic implosion. This implosion is then followed by an expansive magnetic feeling, which occurs when the blissful awareness of the heart merges with the emptiness of mind, revealing to the practitioner a glimpse of the eternal light of the universe, of Tao, hidden within his or her own heart. It is like a tube torus, a sacred geometric formation. The central core of the torus is centripetal, pulling in and imploding light, while the periphery of the tube torus is centrifugal, pushing out the magnetic field of the implosion only to again be pulled in, creating a continuous balance and harmony between two opposing forces. It is very similar to a black hole creating an event horizon to a point of singularity where all things become possible.

Once again, *Mind is Gravity* is an important phrase and meditation that can reveal some great truths, especially to those who need to perfect their lower or negative emotions. Remember that as you embrace the feminine nature within yourself, your emotions refine themselves easily and the body and spirit become calm, and is a result of you doing this work and *living* this art. The outer world will change along with the new internal changes. Just remember, change must first occur within. In order to change the outside, mind is the key to the mergence and balance of the micro and macrocosms, the universe inside and outside.

You may be asking, "Now that I have united with the male and female essence within myself, what will the next step be?" Well, to put it simply, you should now unify with the universe around you. And how is that done? By seeing that the world and all it contains are part of you. I don't mean in terms of thought, but by actually extending your magnetic energy generated by practicing the KUNLUN System into nature and feeling the living force around you.

Lose yourself, and nature will begin to speak to you. After a while, you will feel this unique, lively sensation and you may ask yourself, "How do I unite myself as one with nature even deeper?" Try this meditative approach, which should be done from your own heart.

When you look at an object, do not label it as to what it is, just observe it without giving it a label. The reason for this is that labeling anything you observe gives it more power and solidness within your own mind. However, if you look at it as a simple image of the mind with no attachment or label, the object of observation loses its power over you, so the more you become unattached to the image, the more power you regain and the more free the mind and heart become. You will begin to see what is projecting the image of the object within your mind, and you will see the dance of energy that projected the image within your eyes, because you are no longer just looking, you are now seeing. Again, the receptive female mind and heart, especially for us men, will greatly increase the abilities of spirit to manifest for us. This is what I call entering onto the path of doing without doing.

# Chapter Three

## *What is the KUNLUN System?*

I have had many great teachers throughout my life, including Taoist teachers, Tibetan lamas, Hawaiian kahunas, and shamans from the Navaho and Apache traditions. It is from my broad studies and life experiences, including several near death experiences, that I developed the KUNLUN System, the *path of no more learning*, the form becoming formless. I named it KUNLUN System in order not to favor an individual teacher but to embrace them all.

The Kunlun Mountains, the home of the immortals, drew me when I was young, as my teachers always spoke about the place where the great immortals lived and taught people the ways of awakening. The teachings from the Kunlun Mountains represent the downward flow, the path of water, and a reflection of the practice of reversing the waterwheel, which is the journey of man becoming celestial, much as the knowledge of reversing the flow of life from within, and was also called the Secret of the Golden Flower. Cultivated inner power is the emanation of the gifts of spirit within our heart. With this understanding, combined with the grace of my teachers' life knowledge, I have created this system so that it would be understandable and accessible to those who searched for their own wisdom, only found within themselves.

I learned the various traditions from my teachers but felt that for the western mind, many of the teachings contained a lot of dogma that we, in the west, could not really understand. So through my life experiences, knowledge, and ability to see the energy body, I was able to refine the teaching, taking out what was not needed but at the same time preserving the essence of the traditional practices. Through this system, the art spread quickly throughout the world because of its simple and direct approach. To this day, you will find this art being practiced throughout the world. From the Tibetan nuns in Burma, down into Africa, all the way through Europe, and into the United States and Canada, just to name a few places.

Why did this art spread throughout our world so quickly? Because it opened up a part of us that we had forgotten — that part within ourselves wanting to express itself from both the inside and outside as to *who* we truly are. This desire to know our true essence is within the mind matrix of all of us, held in our very *junk* DNA, to know what our own true essence and life purpose was to become.

We become self-aware when our practice and desire merge with the divine plan or essence. This is what I call the *One Law* of nature, the *One Law* of Tao. Everything in the world, from the smallest particle to the biggest object, is connected and enriched by this *One Law*. It is the living life force that runs through and around all things. When you see it energetically through the *sky eye*, part of its manifestation looks like a big multi-colored spider web vibrating with life and color. These lines connect all things both seen and un-seen. If you recall, this is what I had mentioned earlier about our connectedness to all things. These energetic bands are everywhere, emanating from every object and every being, connecting with the sacred source within each, and in our case the very center of our being within the heart, the *wish-fulfilling gem*.

I often say to my friends and students on the path of self-discovery, when you do the practices of the KUNLUN System with the receptive feelings of the heart and a child-like curiosity, through direct experience you will start to have what I call *the drop entering into the ocean of divine wisdom.* New awareness and manifestations will occur naturally when you are ready. Please have no attachment and avoid grasping for these unique spiritual experiences or they will simply disappear until the mind is again receptive, open, ready, and unattached to them.

When you actually begin practicing the form of the KUNLUN System called the KUNLUN Method, you will find it to be a key to accessing the *One Law* of nature. The hidden universe within yourself, your life force, will in time activate and align the body, mind, and spirit with the *One Law.* During your practice time, which will last about one hour, many things will take place at the body, mind, and spiritual levels within you. Just remember non-attachment and merely allow your mind to observe the direct experience. The self is the key, but also of great importance is to experience the work from within your heart, not your head.

During your practice, your body may sweat a lot or you may feel a lot of heat both inside and out, especially during the earlier stages of this practice. Please remember, this is a stage of purification in which the generated biological and light energy is removing both physical and energetic blocks, respectively. This happens regardless of wherever these blocks may be located within you. Eventually you may feel very cold at times, but this is nothing to worry about, as it is a sign that the body is simply becoming more magnetic as your bio-energy and light energy flow increases within your body. I was once told by a scientist that by practicing this method, it is possible for the body to become super-conductive at room temperature. This is a very interesting thought to ponder and is directly related to the braiding of the DNA during bliss implosion discussed earlier.

During your practice, you also may laugh and cry for no reason. Do not worry; these expressions are simply one way of balancing the emotions. As the emotions arise, they come into their own balance through the energy flowing from the nerves to the various organs that hold those emotions, and a connection is being created between the mundane mind of the head and the perfected mind within the heart. My advice is to let the emotions flow, and above all, remember the great secret: smile, smile, smile.

Smiling serves many purposes. First and foremost, it opens the crown energy and opens the skull bones, which should be freely moving, much the same way as when we were infants. Smiling also lightens and lifts the organs within your body, freeing them from the pull of gravity. So instead of feeling the heavy feeling from not smiling, you can choose to be lighter within yourself, beginning with smiling. Try this: simply smile from the heart and study the resultant feelings you experience within yourself. Then frown and notice the results, especially when you do the KUNLUN Method. You will soon notice how your experiences will be amplified during and after practicing the KUNLUN Method. You can trust that your experiences will be more pleasant when keeping the gentle smile of the Buddha or Quan Yin on your face. This smile says, "I see the light within; may I take you there?"

After beginning the method, it is common and most likely that your legs will bounce or shake, your body may start to sway, or your arms will start to do their own motions. Just let it all happen by itself, and if your arms break posture, it is okay because once you start the movements you do not have to hold the KUNLUN Method posture, as it mainly serves to start the energy moving. You may also take different spontaneous yogic postures. Again, let it happen without your mind making up the movements. Simply smile and with childlike trust and wonder experience from your heart all that occurs. When the blocks for that day are gone, the body will simply stop moving, and at this point, you would end your practice session. Eventually, a time I call the *little death* of the ego-self will come. The body will become blissful, the *sky eye* between the eyebrows will begin to open, and your body may arch backwards.

The outer breath you are normally aware of will become faint, but you will begin an inner breathing, which occurs through the skin itself. The skin takes over and acts like a lung. We call this skin or snake breathing. When this moment of grace occurs, you will experience the taste of the divine light within. This light will be golden white and very bright as though you are traveling through a tunnel into a great vastness of unlimited joy. This is called *merging with the one* or *the drop entering the ocean of wisdom* or simply *immersion*. The light you will see is your own divine essence or seed, hidden within your heart. It is within this moment that your conscious spirit, the I, is now seeing and experiencing this light from the pineal gland awakening from its sleep inside the *crystal palace* and is now looking down through the energetic channel of awakening described earlier as the katika channel, the channel of clarity. So as your spirit travels down through this channel from the crystal palace, the mundane mind sees its own divinity within the heart itself, and the ego and the ego-less mind merge in the blissful ocean of the heart folded inside-out. The blissful nature now creates the tube torus harmonic effect of perfect unity of opposites: implosion and explosion, centripetal and centrifugal force now perfectly balanced in the Tai Chi of infinity, the perfect spin beyond light speed.

Do you know that when you die or have a near-death experience, you travel through this energetic channel back to the source within your own heart? Subsequently, the body loses five ounces of weight when it passes from this world to the next level of awakening. Death is not an ending to all things but another beginning. Death can be looked at as a graduation, a finishing of those lessons we wanted to learn in this life. To me, life is a vacation from the world of spirit, a chance to become physical and to be able to have a limited experience from an unlimited potential. Remember we only take our experiences with us as we continue on the path into the next journey with clarity, thought, and experiences of this life. My teachers once said to me awakening can come three different ways. The first way is after leaving the body and the physical world, a natural death, so to speak. The limitation is that you cannot get your full awakening without your body, as it is the reflection of the experiences, positive and negative, learned through this life. It is part of our original mind, but we leave part of our self behind, making this an incomplete union of the whole mind. The second way of awakening is at the moment of change between the levels of life and death, the world of the known and unknown. At this important moment, we are too busy with the transition process, so unless we have meditated to be conscious and control our inner energy through preparatory methods relating to this moment of chaotic transition, awakening will be difficult for the average person. Now the third possibility is to have the spiritual awakening before the death process occurs. This is for those who wish to be of service to the universe and to all the beings within it. It is said that those who hold back their own enlightenment for the benefit of others were on a greater path of serving, becoming the servers of the garden, the bodhisattvas of Earth. My teachers also said that death was the greatest form of mind limiting itself because when death occurs we outright refuse to change ourselves. In essence, our ability to transform beyond the speed of light, beyond the energy of light, beyond the emptiness becomes self-limiting upon our physical death.

Death, in its simplest state, is the death all must face one day, but in the spiritual death, the ancients could pick when, where, and how they would leave this world. Some would choose to leave the body behind, while others would take the body with them. The ancients knew that our mind was the key to understanding the secrets, hidden and reflected by nature, that are all around us but unnoticed by the mundane mind. The mundane mind affects the energetic body and the physical body through outer experiences. The masters understood that negative emotions indeed affect the outcome of awakening the body of light, even neutralized the process, while the positive emotions quickened the path towards the great body of light emanation.

We human beings should take notice of the words of the ancients who attained the great body of light. They would tell us that we choose our own destiny, its outcome, and we alone are responsible for what occurs on that path. Our choices and way of living in the present dictate the possibilities of our future.

All living things are allotted the same amount of heartbeats in their lifetimes here on the earthly plane. We as human beings can change this aspect because we are conscious, able to change aspects of our life, and able to decide consciously or subconsciously how long or short we live in this life.

I like to use the metaphor of the hummingbird and the turtle to illustrate how we can either lengthen or shorten our lives. Those on the path of the hummingbird grasp all things and move quickly, burning their allotted heartbeats, therefore shortening their lives. As normal human beings, we do this during the day, becoming in essence the spirit of the hummingbird, and when we return home from work we find ourselves exhausted with no energy to do other things except to eat and sleep, and sleeping a lot because of the need of our exhausted body to regenerate for another day of hummingbird action. The organs act like capacitors, which hold the energy for the brain to work, and when one organ becomes depleted, the corresponding organs' emotions become affected, and this leads in most cases to rising imbalances in body, mind, or spirit.

Now if we can learn to be as a turtle, we can lengthen and easily sustain our lives with more time for more experiences to have while we are in the physical body. Turtle, by its nature, is very smart. It reserves its energy and does not waste itself or its life force on useless endeavors, and it lives a very long time. You will also find that as a turtle-type person you will start to slow down, enjoying the simplicity of life more. So in our art, be as a turtle, live long and be well. By simplifying your everyday life and making the KUNLUN System a part of your routine, and living every moment like it is your first and your last, life can and will reveal its greatness to you because you are living in harmony with nature and the universe.

## The Journey Toward the Diamond Body or Gold Dragon Body

On our journey, the practices will allow us to reach towards the ultimate spiritual goal, the attainment of the living body of light. In the Taoist understanding, it is called the indestructible diamond body attainment, and in the Tibetan Buddhist tradition, it is called the great rainbow body emanation. In the new-age understanding, it is also called the light body. What it boils down to is that the KUNLUN System, through meditative and breathing techniques, facilitates the complete opening of the energy body, including the chakras, energy meridians, and three specific energy storage areas called dantiens. This ancient phenomenon of opening through these techniques allows for the purification of body, mind, and spirit. When this opening occurs, there is a spontaneous critical energy accumulation within the body's energetic field that reflects deeply into the gross matter of the physical body. This causes an alchemical transmutation of the physical body into a more-refined, less-dense structure. Scientists have found that human DNA can itself emit coherent light similar to a laser.

With this in mind, imagine that every cell with its DNA starts to harmonize in resonance together. This is done by the cell nucleus feeling the sounds of the heart when the heart is experiencing the plasma bliss of the opening of the katika channel. These unique and qualified overtones of love and compassion from the heart cause braiding of the DNA strands together, individually and collectively, embedding upon themselves non-destructively, creating a uniquely tuned antenna that guides and directs the potential energy of the quantum field into and through the whole organism. This causes the entire organism to be in complete harmony and thus unified within itself. This unity creates a coherent entity, able to super-conduct light energy at room temperature and, subsequently, the human body starts to emit light, openly and profoundly. When all of these cells and energy of the universe are fully attuned, they resonate harmoniously at the single frequency of the *One Law* of the universe. This concept also relates to all traditions stating that the spiritually ready person, who has prepared correctly will go through this process of ultimate awakening, appearing to a sensitive person or to a person whose *sky eye* is open, as an intense, blinding light. There are various forms of awakening found throughout our world, but in this particular method, enlightenment means to emanate the spiritual light from within the body or microcosm into the macrocosm. This is the level where one would then teach in presence without the need for word.

In tradition, when the student was ready, the energetic reflection of such an awakened teacher who has attained the indestructible diamond body or gold dragon body would cause a quickening of spirit within the ready student. This was known as teaching in presence. Another means of creating the necessary mind training is to meditate on the concept of *Mind is Gravity*. This form of thought or meditation allows you to learn and experience non-attachment, which would naturally lead into emptiness, and when the blissful awareness of KUNLUN Energy merges with the emptiness of mind within the heart, awakening naturally occurs.

When I was creating this system from the various methods of awakening, I learned from my many teachers; they agreed that ninety percent of purification was actually the balancing and refinement of the mundane mind. The focus on positive virtues such as love, humility, compassion, and joy was, and still is, paramount in awakening. Focusing on the negative virtues, such as anger, greed, inflated ego, and wanting for power, are thought to completely stop the process of purification of awakening.

As you might have figured out, the body is a mere reflection of the positive and negative virtues and experiences from life. The body reflects these qualities as good health and well being or sickness based on the virtues that the person decides to cultivate. So on this path you may just wish to practice the primary methods to become aware of the hidden potentials within your body and just develop certain qualities, such as good health or mental well being; but if you seek to travel the road of awakening, the virtues are important to understand and master. As you start to reflect on this possibility, you may ask yourself why were you born and what is your great purpose for being here and now. Why are you reading this book? Is it fate or is it by choice? One question may lead to ten thousand more questions, so in practice, surrender any questions and trust that they will be answered from within.

Very few people ponder life's true spiritual meaning. Mostly, they seek something in the moment, but never really contemplate why they wish it and for what end it serves. Have you ever seriously thought about what you were seeking to attain at the end of the path? Why do I ask this question? If you truly know what it is you are seeking spirit wise, then the path and the world of spirit will supply the necessary experiences for you to attain those goals; if you walk the path humbly and seek to help those less fortunate, then wonderful things become noticeable to you and those around you.

Part of what motivated me on the path was seeking the direct experience. To me, this meant not just listening to my teachers and taking what they said as truth, but to also learn from my own direct experience through diligent practice. In truth, my goal was to go further than my teachers had gone. I was once told that a true teacher would teach his or her students with a fullness of spirit, which meant that if you really taught them correctly, one day the student would surpass the teacher and whatever the teacher had attained spiritually. This would allow the art to express more fully with each generation, as long as the original methods were not diluted, and the arts of awakening would grow and change with the times. Some arts flourished for a time, while other systems and their methods slowly disappeared. How could this occur? Imagine the following scenario.

It is typical, historically, that when a teacher died, the senior student became the new master, taking over the school and its teachings. The new self-ascribed master believed that he or she had the complete teachings and knowledge of the now deceased master. The new teacher withheld something from his student, just as the previous master kept something from him, and eventually the art would become less and less complete, with each generation of master keeping a little for himself, until the essence was forgotten over many generations. Many ancient methods of awakening have died out because teachers kept the next generation of students from learning the complete system, fearing either abuse or change from the system's original purpose. There is, of course, logic to this understanding, but since time is changing and human beings are awakening, this is the time I feel all masters should share what they know to help the world and its people become more awakened.

Your human body is a miracle of the universe, with the great mysteries housed within it. You *are* the universe. You are the essence of living light, slowed down into the physical manifestation of frozen light. When we do our practices, we are speeding ourselves back up into the sacred vibration of truth, even beyond the speed of light, and in the process, remembering who and what we truly are and what we came here to do.

# Chapter Four

## *The Refined KUNLUN Method Posture with Yin/Yang Hand*

The first step on your new path of self-discovery is to realize that just getting to the end of the ultimate journey of self-realization is not what is most important. Rather, as you are on the path in your everyday life, consider this: you are now walking backwards, returning to source. Taoist philosophy reminds us that to become full, we must become empty. In order to go forward, we must go back. This is the *doing without doing.* As you continue on your path, do not be content to just practice the arts of KUNLUN System, instead, strive to *live* the art, in every wakened and sleeping moment, *feel* it in every breath. This is *living* the art of awakening. This is not a path of *if, and, but,* or *maybe,* but rather, a *do* or *do not* journey. Living your art means to embrace and embody positive virtues, such as love, humility, compassion, and joy, every day. With this in mind, let us continue the path together.

### Preparation for Your Practice

An important part of any practice is developing the proper mind set. As you prepare to do your practice, try to leave work at the door; allow the worries of the day to stay outside your practice time. Have a child-like, playful nature. Try emulating nature by being in the moment, allowing the busy mind within your head to gently drop into the quiet place of the heart. With this gentle, playful mindset, you will be ready to explore the universe within.

I recommend that you create a place of sacredness, a special spot only for you, where you can surrender yourself at the door of spiritual experience. This will be your place of communication with the divine spirits of the unseen world.

For the KUNLUN Method practice, you will need loose clothing. You will also need a comfortable wood chair or seat, preferably one without arms and backrest. When sitting at the edge of your chair, it should be of the height where your hips are slightly higher than your knees. Avoid using a metal chair. A sturdy wood chair is preferable. It is a good idea to place cushions on the floor around you just in case, during those times of sudden grounding, you fall off your chair. Placing your chair upon carpet, a yogic mat, or an animal skin is a good way to insulate the increased energy within the body created during practice and to keep it from transferring into the Earth. You may also place an animal fur on top of your chair if you wish. The animal skin on the chair or floor or rubber mat on the floor allows the increase in refined electrical aspects of the body to stay within the body and its etheric field. This will support the building of the field without draining out the additional and refined flowing current within the energetic channels into the Earth. The insulation effect of the mat or fur also allows the magnetic potential within the body to be isolated, and as it grows stronger within the body during practice, it will connect and ground with the life-force of the Earth. The mat or fur will help maintain a clean magnetic field until such a time when the Earth's magnetic field must unite and tie into the magnetic field of the body. This naturally happens as greater and greater coherence and harmony at the cellular level of the body occurs during practice. This is similar to the raindrop becoming the ocean. The body's magnetic field becomes part and parcel to the Earth's magnetic field. And the more magnetic field available, the greater capacity to move and carry the electrical charge. Magnetic vectors of greater gauss intensity naturally create or implore scalar and electrical charge, which increases potential energy in the body. "Live long and prosper" as the starship *Enterprise*, your universal vehicle, the body, goes into warp drive. Grounding our bodies is very important. I always say to my friends the higher the tree wishes to grow, the deeper the roots must be within the Earth.

Music is an integral part of this system, especially in the beginning, as it helps in developing a less-controlling, more surrendering mind. If you are very calm, try using music that gets you motivated, like Mongolian throat singing. If you are not an emotional person, try listening to the Japanese musician Kitaro, whose music evokes deep feeling. Eventually, when you have reached a very peaceful, calm state and can enter into stillness, let the use of music go and listen to the sounds within you. Listen to the sound and vibration of the heart, or the sounds within the ear, and try following the sound back to its source.

## KUNLUN Method

The main posture, known as the KUNLUN Method, is the key to the *One Law* of nature: the law that demonstrates that all things are connected through and accessed by the loving nature of the heart. As you become more open and sensitive to the *One Law*, remember, it is important to *play* with the energy. Play with a childlike nature; do not try to control the essence of nature.

Now that you have created your special sacred space, make the light gentle and dim so you will not get distracted by bright light. Remove all breakable and sharp-pointed items away from your practice area. Sit quietly in your chair and allow yourself to become open, surrendering the tensions of the outside world. Generate your childlike nature, allowing your mind to drop into the awaiting heart. Your eyes should be open halfway, your mouth closed, but the jaw loose. Simply breathe gently in and out through the nose equally, without a break or space in between the breathing in and out.

This is what we called the *One Breath* method and it is an excellent warm-up for your practice. If you do this correctly, your breathing will come only from the lower abdomen and not from the chest. The abdomen should begin to feel warm, the heart will start to feel calm, and the mind will naturally become empty. Continue this breathing until you feel connected in body, mind, and spirit. Now turn on your selected music and sit down on your chair.

Remember to smile. Smiling is very important because it opens the crown and lifts the organs and the heart, allowing freedom from the gravity of Earth and of a heavy mind. The smile, you will find, is taught in all Taoist traditions and is considered an important attribute in learning the way of Tao. Think of this in another way: when you were born, your skull at the crown was open, allowing the cosmic flow of life to come through the top of the head. But as we developed, we lost this union, as the crown slowly closed up. The only time it opens again is through spiritual practice or at the moment of death. So "smile, smile, smile" is your mantra for the basic work ahead.

We have now set our mind to its proper nature; we have balanced and unified the body, mind, and spirit through the *One Breath*, and have connected all of this through the inner and outer action and sensation of smiling. It is now time to learn the posture.

Remove your shoes and let your bare feet touch the ground, mat, or fur. Sit on the edge of your wooden chair with your legs shoulder width apart. Now arch your low back very slightly. Not too much, though, as we do not want our back slumping forward like the posture of an old dragon. Place your right palm at the heart level in front of your chest, palm facing down.

Look at your right palm and allow the fingers to be slightly straightened, just until you feel a slight tension within the palms. This action opens the palm hearts of your hands. The middle and ring finger should be more relaxed than the others, and should be pointing downward slightly. Let the wrist naturally relax downward, allowing the right hand to hang with ease.

Let us now work on the left hand position. Put the hand in front of the lower abdomen in a palm up position. Remember not to rest the palm on your lap, it must be held up gently above the lap. Your left palm should be slightly stretched to feel a slight tension within the palms. When you feel this, allow the middle finger to be more relaxed and curved than the other fingers. There is no break in the wrist. The wrist and hand are in alignment horizontally, unlike the right hand, which has a natural drop or break.

Now with the proper hand positions in place, align both palms at the centerline of the body with the hands floating in front of their designated areas. Let your head and neck become comfortably straight with the spine. Slightly lift the top of your head towards the sky to feel the back of the neck stretch, and then relax as much as you can. *The posture you are now holding is the key to self-awakening.*

Now, to activate the process of self-awakening, simply lift your heels off the ground and extend the ankles, but not to the point of locking them. This foot action is the on-off switch for the posture. Now, let the mind *go* and become formless, without attachment, and let the process of purification begin. You now have the basic instructions to begin the path, which can at times be quiet and at other times full of action and movement. The key is to trust the process and let your body guide your feeling and subsequent movement. As the mind empties, the body will know exactly what to do to attain self-awakening. Remember, it is all good.

After about one hour of practicing the KUNLUN Method, the body will come back to normal by itself. If you wish to close down your practice before that time, simply ask yourself to slow down. Lower your feet, placing them flat on the ground. Smile, and comfortably sit back in your chair with your mind resting lightly within your heart. Allow the built-up energy from the practice to gently flow down behind the belly button with the mind gently guiding it to its storage point behind the belly button. This is where the accumulated energy should always be stored. Place your hands on your belly with the left hand over right, both palms facing towards the belly button. When you feel back to normal after sitting in this quiet position, end your practice for the day.

Remember, when you have completed your practice for the day, never, ever, does the accumulated energy stay in your head. The energy must always be stored in the lower dantien, using the close down method described above, and your mantra

**KUNLUN Method Side View**

**KUNLUN Method Front View**

should be "smile, smile, smile" and "ground, ground, ground."

If you are serious about awakening, this method is an effective standalone practice. Practicing this art once a day for five days is enough. Taking two days off per week will help you to stay in balance with the mundane world.

This path is uniquely and profoundly water, the downward flow of Heavenly Way. It is extremely important not to mix the KUNLUN System and KUNLUN Method with practices related to the fire path traditions. Avoid combining with forceful methods — such as kundalini, which is a fiery, upward path of energy flow — with the downward flow and water way. Look at it this way, if there are two trains on the same track coming from opposite directions, it will lead to a crash. You want to avoid this.

If you are a fire path practitioner and you wish to try the KUNLUN System practices, then I advise you to discontinue the fire practices for three months, giving yourself this time to fully experience the path of the water way. At the end of this three-month period, you will need to make a decision about which path is correct for you, as I do not recommend combining these opposite paths and flows of energy. If you are uncertain about a specific practice, then simply avoid doing it. I call the KUNLUN System the *path of no more learning* for a very good reason, which you will discover and understand as you progress through the different levels of your own divine awakening.

**Eye and Tongue Positions**

In our tradition, there are several refinements that help facilitate the awakening experience. One of the refinements involves the position in which one holds the eyes during meditation and spiritual practice. You will find that eye positions may vary from tradition to tradition; however, I suggest that you allow your eyes to be in the half open, half closed position during your practice. This relaxed focus is symbolic of walking between the worlds and will lead you into the half-awake, half-asleep state of mind. I suggest looking over the nose instead of at the tip of the nose, while using a gentle, soft focus, which will prevent tension from building up in the eyes and eye muscles. During practice, the eyes will move in different directions by themselves, especially during the purification stage, so just let things happen as they naturally arise. Your eyes have a tendency to do their own thing once you activate, so just let things happen and allow them to move without your controlling mind getting in the way of the process. In other words, surrender to the nature of Tao within. I cannot stress this enough to you.

Another refinement involves the position in which one holds the tongue during practice. Tongue positions are an important part of making the internal arts work. For example, when you do the Five Elements practice, if you let your tongue touch naturally behind the front upper teeth, you will allow the five elements to combine with the energy of the microcosmic flow. This flow is electrical in nature and is represented by the in and out breath of polarity, and is also known as the *path of man*. This point behind the front teeth is a fire point in our specific art. For the KUNLUN Method, allow the tip of your tongue to touch the highest part of the palate at the roof of the mouth. This point is called the *door of water* and allows the magnetic current created from your practice to flow into the upper dantien or *crystal palace* within the skull.

During your practices, your tongue may spontaneously change position or you may notice that the tip of your tongue moves back to the *door of air,* the place where the hard and soft palate meet. If your tongue goes way up the back of your throat, it may try to worm its way upward towards the brain. This movement is called mahamudra in some traditions. If it occurs, it may catch you by surprise, but do not worry, as your body has all the understanding of this process built in, and when you are ready, such things will occur naturally, without the mundane mind getting in the way.

If you are not sure where to position your tongue, you can ask yourself a few simple questions to determine which position is right for you. Do you know what your tendency is regarding nature's five elements? What type of personality are you? Are you a fire-type person, a water-type person, or an air-type person? If you are a fire-type person, you may be someone who is not patient or perhaps you have done other practices relating to fire. If so, allow the tongue tip to touch the highest part of the upper palate. This is the water point that allows the energy to awaken the *crystal palace* and glands of the upper dantien in the head area. If you are a water-type person who is outgoing and not scholarly or is someone who is centered in their heart and heart feelings, I would advise to let the tongue sit naturally behind the front teeth. This point represents the path of fire and will help loosen your body, generate heat, and allow the body to physically and energetically purify. If you are the air-type person, one who has an empty mind, place the tongue where the hard and soft palate meet, so that there is balance between the emptiness of the mind and the unobstructed flow of energy flowing within the body. This point and tongue position leads to the union of form and formlessness within.

In most traditions, the placement of the tip of the tongue varies depending on the system and the master who may give or vary specific positions of the tongue based on the practices and the desired effect. For example, in most people, the tongue naturally touches behind the upper front teeth. This tongue position allows the inner energy to flow through a route called the microcosmic flow. This energy route is commonly used by many energy practitioners in China. This flow is important in the steps leading to awakening and is perfect for developing healing ability, martial arts, and spiritual endeavors. This microcosmic orbit usually flows up the back, flowing around the skull, then down the front to the point the circulation had started, usually the lower dantien. Flow in this direction is more the fire path.

There is also a water path of counter circulation that flows in the opposite direction, but eventually both directions will flow at the same time, opening a new door of awareness. If you think about it for one moment, when two flows are going opposite each other, like two waves identical but opposite, merging, they neutralize each other. In a sense, this merging creates a space of neutrality, and in this space of neutrality is where we find the zero point potential from the quantum field, which we as energy practitioners can tap into.

In essence, the microcosmic flow that starts in the lower dantien and flows around the pelvic floor up the spine along the conception vessel, over the top of the skull, down the front of the body along the governing vessel and back to the lower dantien is the element of fire and is reflective of Earth. The microcosmic flow that starts at the lower dantien and moves up the governing vessel, over the top of the skull, down the spine, along the conception vessel, and around the floor of the pelvis back to the lower dantien is the element of water, and its path reflects the Human Being at the heart level. This is the water path of love and compassion.

The combination of the two opposite microcosmic flows, water and fire together, provides a new element, the super-heated steam that is the gaseous state of water with high kinetic energy transferred from fire. This super-heated steam can now fill the upper dantien, which is the air element of Heaven, consisting of the neck, skull cavity, and brain, and provide that kinetic energy to the etheric light centers of the brain, such as the pituitary and pineal gland, the third eye or *crystal palace,* and the cerebrospinal fluid. The super-heated steam is a metaphor for the zero point potential from the quantum field and also is fundamental to the bliss plasma vapor filling the katika channel to the heart center, the essence of what it is to be Human. As the kinetic energy of the neutrino sea, caused by the resonance of the zero point field, comes into the brain, the Elixir of Life or Amrita is created by specific brain components and is circulated through the entire body via the cerebrospinal fluid, through the peripheral and autonomic nervous systems, and eventually to each cell in the body. This will create the immortal alchemy that is the foundation of all Taoist teachings.

The clear and simple message here is that the Human, in all glory of the heart, connects Heaven and Earth through the creation of the super-heated steam or zero point energy that invites Heaven and Earth to play with and for each other for the mutual benefit of all. We are indeed the stewards that make this possible. In this art, you are learning both microcosmic routes intuitively. It is not required to practice each individually because the routes will start to flow more naturally as we release the negativities of our mind. Removal of blockages via this unique method allows these energy routes to flow unhindered. The results should be noticeable as you continue your journey. Just be patient.

## Jaw Position

With regard to the jaw position, we should smile softly with mouth closed, and the jaw hanging loosely, just as we do with the *One Breath*. This alignment allows the sutures of the skull to readjust their position to properly realign and break the calcifications of the skull during the practice of this system.

## Effects and Manifestations of the KUNLUN Method

Before you sit and do your first practice, let us talk about the many possible manifestations that can occur during the KUNLUN Method practice. It is also important to know that it is not unusual for many changes and manifestations to occur after the practice has ended. Understand that the changes are simply a part of the journey.

The obvious manifestation is the shaking of the legs, which occurs when the energy is starting to activate through the legs. This movement empowers the kidneys and activates the sacral pump by breaking any sacral calcifications. This movement also allows the pineal gland and pituitary gland of the brain to begin communicating with each other. Some people will move gently in the beginning while others will have stronger, more active movement. The movement signifies purification of the mind, qi, energy centers, and pathways at various levels and allows for the opening of dormant or stuck energy within the energetic and physical body. Some of us have a lot to get rid of while others have little. As your body completely clears, and the movement ceases, stillness will occur as your body systems balance both physically and energetically.

Don't be concerned if you have no movement in the beginning. Some people have movement in the beginning before reaching the stillness phase, while others go from emptiness to movement. Again, don't worry about it, just allow things to naturally happen, and if you have no movement, sit quietly, embrace the emptiness, and let your mind watch without control. You will also need to *feel* more and think less to really experience the depth of this art. And remember, above all, smile and remain in your heart.

You may experience an increase or decrease in body temperature during times of physical purification. At times, you may feel very hot as the organs purify and the electrical force within the nerves quicken. At other times, a cold, magnetic feeling will occur as your channels, such as the central channel or thrusting channel, awaken with the energy being generated. You may feel energy rising up your spine or flowing down your spine. The microcosmic orbit may activate and the tongue may quiver from the energy.

You may also feel great happiness or sadness as the energy comes out of duality and into oneness. You may see or experience lights of different colors or intensities as the *crystal palace* within the brain awakens. Different tastes, smells, and different spiritual powers also may awaken. Some people speak in tongues, a phenomenon that occurs when the divine potential within your heart starts to communicate with the mundane mind of the head through the katika channel, or channel of clarity, which connects the two. Speaking in tongues can also be thought of as a compressed computer file hidden within the dormant or *junk* DNA. With time, you will be able to access this file, retrieve the new information that at the moment of opening will not yet be understandable to you, and download it into the conscious mind, and you will be able to put the information to good use. Please do not have attachment to any of these sensations and manifestations. Just trust that it is all part of a natural process.

There may be times when you have a difficult block and you find yourself being pulled to the ground by a magnetic force. This force will originate either from inside or outside of you. This is NOT an entity or spirit doing this to you, but rather your own abundant magnetic field increased through the water path, seeking to connect itself to the Earth's magnetic field, completing a loop between Human and Earth. This abundant magnetic field will now power the electrostatic charge held within the body and provide the dynamic electromagnetic force that will be used in the alchemical process of transmutation, health, and longevity, leading to immortality.

Another interesting manifestation that can occur is the opening of the *sky eye* or third eye. In this case, you may experience different colors within the skull at the forehead area. This place at the center of the head is commonly known to Taoists as the crystal palace. This experience occurs when the internal energies start to awaken the important energy source of being within you. Just remember, when this phenomenon occurs, have no attachment to it or it will close.

Do you known that the Mongolian shamans believe in ninety-nine different worlds and Tengri, or spirits, that live in those unseen worlds. Just think what interesting things one may see after a long time of practicing! I suggest that you learn to observe, without attachment, any manifestations that may arise. Remember it is only the beginning, the first page on this new journey, which later may connect into the *wisdom eye* of the ancients.

As the *sky eye* opens, you may experience pressure in the sutures or forehead. When this pressure occurs, one way to help yourself is to rub your scalp briskly with your fingers, then rub the ears with the palms until they get red and hot. This massage will release the trapped blood within the brain and relax the tension in the skull. The pressure in your skull is from the magnetic energy generated by the stimulated brain and cerebrospinal fluid trying to circulate and clear out the sutures of the skull. You will also notice an increase in the intracranial pressure and the head shape expanding and contracting at one time or another. These are all normal processes that may occur while doing this work.

Another experience you may have in addition to seeing intense light is that you may feel and taste a sweet, honey-like fluid in your mouth. This elixir comes from either the back of the throat or from the upper palate as the suture located in that region loosens and excretes due to the work you are doing with the practices. This is the pure essence from the glands of the *crystal palace* located within the brain. This liquid is usually thick in nature, smooth in texture, and has a fragrance of roses, lavender, or something very pleasant. When this *ambrosia* occurs, and after the mouth becomes full of this soma, mix it with a gulp of air, swish it in the mouth vigorously, and swallow it with a loud gulp. After swallowing, feel it go to your lower abdomen, where it will charge up the lower dantien. The ancients called this special hormonal ambrosia soma or the *elixir of immortality*. It was also called the jade ambrosia, the wish-fulfilling gem, the descent of grace, the anointing and baptism by water, as well as the tear of Ra in the Egyptian tradition.

Some people see images of nagas or snakes, which are nothing to fear as they simply represent the spiraling forces of nature hidden within and around us all the time. This symbology is found throughout the world in every mystical tradition. This ageless image represents how the unknowing mind reflects and tries to understand these different forms of energy.

When it comes time to experience the *great time of tasting* or test of letting go of *I,* or the ego, you will have a unique experience that will occur when all parts of you are in perfect alignment with the *One Law* of Tao. It is the self-immersing into the joyous waters of blissful awareness.

There will come a time when you will be filled with indescribable bliss, in which there are five levels, based on which chakra is stimulated. The lower chakras will be most intense in sensation and the energy does refine itself as it rises upward, so allow your mind to rest in the heart and not in the lower energy centers during this time. Eventually, when it reaches the heart, you should focus into the sensation of stillness while gently smiling, and as the light appears within the crystal palace, lead the refined bliss into emptiness.

When the mind within your head sinks into the crystal palace, the mundane mind starts to see through the *sky eye* (pineal gland) down through the katika channel, gazing into the divine light of the heart. This experience may be scary at first, but just relax and trust. This is the time when the mundane mind catches a glimpse of its own divinity. This light is the same light that people describe seeing in a near-death experience—the light at the end of the tunnel. What people are actually seeing in the NDE is their mundane mind descending down the katika channel, towards the essence of the Tao hidden within their own hearts. Remember that for everything you seek spiritually, the root and the cause is inside of you. The outside world and all it contains are also reflections of what is inside you.

When you have purified to a certain level within the core of your own being and your glands have regenerated and are full of energy and your mind is settled within your heart, the door of spirit starts to open. Your sun and moon channels responsible for the duality of breathing in and out start to energetically collapse. The outer breath becomes so subtle you barely notice yourself breathing. This is the time to surrender and let go of all fear as the journey is about to get more fascinating.

You may start to feel a magnetic coolness throughout the body as the thrusting channel or central channel starts to activate. When this occurs, the spine will arch and you will be filled with warmth, usually within your heart, and a blissful energy of great expansiveness. Your eyes will roll upward, looking towards the top of the skull or in between the eyebrows, your mouth will open wide, and your outer breath will effortlessly disappear. This blissful experience is what is called the *little death.*

This is the moment that facilitates change and offers us the opportunity to choose to continue on as a normal human being or to become something greater than ourselves. The outer breath will become more subtle and an inner breath will take over. Once you experience this, the skin, which acts like a second lung, activates and you begin to absorb scalar energy through the skin. At this time, remember to SURRENDER and allow the Tao to bring you toward the door of greatness and infinity of being. It is the experience of spiritual transition through this *little death* that allows us to understand the union of self with the divine truth within each one of us. The Tibetan tradition calls this *the drop going into the ocean of wisdom.* This represents your individual self-merging with the higher potential in the vessel of the heart. At times your experiences will be subtle, and at other times they could seem overwhelming. Just remember to have NO attachment and let the body do what it needs to do. Throughout the experience, remember to smile, as this simple action will begin your new life.

When you have such a life-altering experience, it is very important to ground yourself by living fully in the mundane world with your new-found sense of being. Make life your art. See the spirit of awakening in all things great and small. See the light and happy awareness in everything you see, hear, smell, taste, and touch.

It bears repeating that many changes and manifestations can occur. The key is not to be attached to them. As I mentioned, various patterns and flashing of multi-colored lights may occur over time, usually accompanied by various sounds and what others refer to as the *music of the spheres*. Different smells may arise from inside and around us. The body will take various yogic postures as the magnetic and electrical potentials open. At times, we will laugh and cry for no reason. Again, do not worry. Remember, this is just purification and you are not going crazy. Know that you have perfect control over this practice, and you dictate the speed, length, and intensity of your practice. If the energy or movement is ever too fast for you, simply ask yourself to slow down, but never stop the movements abruptly. Never stop quickly and always slow down gently. As you get past the purification phase, the energy will flow in many directions. Sometimes energy will flow upward through the spine and at other times downward through the spine. The direction is based on the state of your mind and body at the time of your practice. As I have stated, the experiences you may potentially have will vary. At times, they will be subtle and other times very powerful. The key to success is to have no attachment to your experiences.

Learn to experience the bliss without attachment, knowing that bliss can be addicting, just like a drug, and seeing how blissful you can get is not the true purpose of the KUNLUN Method and System. Remember to live with the highest possible virtue while in this living body of light. Living in this way is to live the art in fullness, reflecting the values of the great masters who came before us. Releasing both the ego and the desire for popularity, power, fame, and fortune that can be gained through power is most easily done at this time of blissful awareness. Our heart, knowing the truth of who we really are, gently illuminates the falsehoods and lies that the ego has perpetrated on our brain and body. All things become clear. The unique and humble purpose of creating the connection between Heaven and Earth becomes the focus, first and foremost. And in joy, the practitioner proceeds to uncover the divine nature of the Tao within and without.

Countless practitioners of the KUNLUN Method and System have had such remarkable experiences where they realize the greatness and importance of their lives as well as discovering a newly found purpose for their existence. Be in harmony with nature, knowing that all you see outside of your body is indeed an extension of yourself. Realize who you are in this universe: the center, the heart of Tao.

# Chapter Five

## Purification, Emptiness, the Physical Body, and Balancing

I t is understood that purification is of great importance with regard to self-awakening. In my opinion, ninety percent of purification is done through the mind itself, letting go of issues, past and present, and fear of the future or unknowns that have complicated our daily lives. With this in mind, we can accept that the body is a mere reflection of the positive and negative experiences that our mind has learned while incarnated in our physical bodies.

When experiencing the releasing phase of your journey through the practice of the KUNLUN Method, many impurities are discharged through physical movement, vocal expression, and emotional and mental processing. In time, the long-held perceptions and experiences that no longer serve us on our path of awakening are removed. One of the most powerful ways this is occurs is through the spontaneous patterns and movements that our body creates during practice. These patterns and movements are similar to a wet dog that vigorously shakes water off its fur until it feels the weight of the water has been removed. The rapid sideways snake-like patterns of the shaking travel from the head to the pelvis with greater frequency and amplitude until all water waste is removed from the skin and fur. The dog's eyes are usually closed, the lips and ears flap uncontrollably, and the tail whips and shakes until the excess water is completely removed. When the mind releases negativity through these actions created by the flowing internal energy, the body starts to correct the various misalignments that are held inside our body from experiences generated by the mind while it is experiencing the world and its lessons. The importance of this purification, regardless of what level it arises at, must always be reflected by your mind and heart in a positive way. Simply smiling during those difficult purification phases will help with your transformation into your own unlimited potential. These cleansings will occur each time you sit to do the practices. Remember, if something occurs that makes you feel uncomfortable, you can simply ask yourself to slow down. If the movement is too strong, use your mind to change the emerging negativity into something positive. Do this with the will of your mind by reflecting on a happy moment or joyous memory from your life. If you do this correctly, the negativity that has arisen can be changed or transmuted by smiling and focusing on the positive experience. With your mind, you can change the negative elements into healthy laughter and a sensation of joy and bliss. I caution you to have no attachment to the blissful experiences as they naturally occur as you do this method. Movement is purification, and stillness is the door to awakening. This is all happening at the same time. As you let go of something that is affecting you negatively, you will also fill this void with a positive thought or joyful experience.

Let us now address the subject of physical purification. If you have abused your body in the past or present by using drugs or alcohol, or if you have ever incurred an injury, the body will start to release the cause or root of this negativity held within your mind and reflected through the limitations of your body. It is part of the path for us to discover, acknowledge, and change the root within the unconscious mind that has caused the problems that exist within and outside of ourselves. I call this the *dark night in the forest*, and it is something we all must experience. This means that we have to consciously see and remedy the causes of our pain. These pains of experience have always been there within you, but forgotten in the streams of time. Everyone on the true path must eventually face their inner self, even though they may not like what they might see or feel or experience at those moments of purification. Try looking at these thoughts and emotions as mind experiences, a picture of past experience forgotten in the desert of the mind and buried within the sands of the unconscious mind. Do not look at these expressions of self as weaknesses, as if you have flaws, inadequacies, or something that makes you seem less than another person. Remember, everyone has such experiences.

In the Navaho tradition, to be a *real human* means to be *godlike* in a physical form. A real human is considered to be a being who feels all experiences deeply, inside and outside of oneself. True human beings do not ignore or hide from their deep emotions. You, my friend, through this internal cultivation, will realize that you are your own master, your own beginning (Alpha) and end (Omega) on this sacred path. You are the self-awakener from the dreams of self-imposed limitation held within the subconscious and the DNA. The experiences held within the DNA are inherited from the lineage of both your mother and father and contain many experiences that, although they do not belong to us, trigger us into behaviors that are not our own. Transmutation of the DNA through the internally made Elixir of Life as well as the internal alchemy created by the spontaneous movements of the practice, reflecting a substantial increase in the electromagnetic potential, transmute our own DNA into carriers of etheric light providing blessings unimaginable.

My Navaho teacher, who was a medicine man, sat down with me one night next to a fire and looked at me with great sincerity and with a quiet voice said, "One day I hope to become a human being." I pondered the meaning of his words, and even to this day, his words are felt deeply within me. This is a great teaching through such simple words. I repeat this story and this phrase to you, my friend, with the hope that you will allow this understanding to sink deeply into your mind. I would like you to think about this concept, this expression, and consider what it means to be a *human being*, and what the purpose is for us being here on this planet. It is not the outside world that makes you a human being. It is the hidden potential and inner greatness waiting to bloom like a lotus growing toward the surface of a muddy pond, emerging to meet the life-giving light of the sun.

I would like for you to remember and use the mantra *Mind is Gravity* whenever you feel stuck. These three simple words provide a reflection, a mirror of the mind that teaches and demonstrates to your conscious mind what holds itself within this world of limitation. If you focus lightly on this mantra while observing your surroundings without label or attachment, you will begin to understand this concept within your own conscious reality and your place in the seen and unseen worlds.

During times of purification, when you are practicing the KUNLUN Method, you may sweat a lot. If you notice that the odor is terrible, this means that toxins are being released. If the scent is highly fragrant and very pleasing, this means the qi is purified. It has been noticed that high-level masters of the past emitted these pleasant fragrances from their body during their teachings. If your perspiration is fragrant, I suggest saving this energy by rubbing it back into the skin when you are finished with your practice. As for using herbs for purification, please use common sense. When using herbal remedies, remember more is not necessarily better. Trust your feelings and your body. If you have doubt, find someone trained in the proper ways of nutrition and herbal medicine to help you.

You may feel more open while under the influence of drugs or alcohol, but by combining the KUNLUN System with mind-altering substances, there is a price to pay for such behavior. Visions come at the price of closing the mingmen point, the gate of life. This mingmen point is our biologic timer, the gate of water related to our kidneys, which need to be nurtured, not abused. Indulging in such substances not only harms the organ systems of the body, it also makes the pineal and other glands disharmonize until they regenerate themselves back to their normal state of activity. So, for your health and longevity, keep a clear mind, gentle focus, and a harmonious body, and you will keep the gate of life or mingmen open.

Having a cloudy mind compromised by psychoactive drugs closes the mingmen more quickly. When the mingmen closes, the subtle energy needed to support the mind through a har-monized, electrically balanced and clear-functioning brain is reduced. This has a direct and limiting effect upon the body's physiologic and mystical processes. Once again, don't over indulge in strong alcohol or take drugs or psychedelic medi-cines because one needs a clear mind by virtue of a balanced brain and heart when working toward their own awakening. Remember that the clouded mind sees nothing but the illusion-ary light that deflects the human being from the path of the clear light within the heart.

## Emptiness

What is emptiness? Based on the KUNLUN System tradition, it can mean many things. To me, emptiness refers to the purified mind that is non-attached to the mental reflections occurring at any given moment. This is what some call *naked awareness*. It is the mind, free of trappings and distractions. While in the moment, if the mind is experiencing total freedom from any bondage, emptiness is like the never-ending blue sky. To me, emptiness also reflects the notion that all things are simply holograms or thought forms within the unattached mind. It is also the un-manifested potential and possibility, the door to unseen elements of the Tao, the great mystery inside and outside of us.

There also exists the *illusionary emptiness*, which is expressed by the mind asking the question to its self: Am I truly empty? Well my friend, if you are asking yourself this question, you have not attained true emptiness. If you get stuck at this level of self-reflection, filled with the doubt of accomplishing the goal, simply empty yourself of the emptiness. Emptiness is the fullness of things within the mind. Form is emptiness and emptiness is form; it is all part of life. If thoughts come to you during your practice, do not ignore them, just allow them to enter into the observing mind and just let those images flow through you without grasping them. With time, they will naturally fade away.

In my younger days of training, I was told that the fears I felt and yet resisted mentally would take on physical form within the dream state. I was told not to run away from the fear because it gives the fear more density, a life of its own. Your subconscious gives this unknown mind element a form, so your conscious mind can understand the root or essence of that hidden fear within the subconscious. My teachers told me not to run away from this subconscious creation, but to turn toward it and hold it consciously with your heart. Grab it even if it struggles to free itself from your grip. Then when both your conscious mind and the identified hidden fear merge into nonduality, it will disappear like incense smoke, freeing you from the bonds of the fearful mind.

As time goes by, you will eventually attain what I call the no-mind state, the naturally attained stillness in which you cannot even generate a thought unless you are interacting with another person. You will be living and breathing within the total present moment, free of attachment to all things, ideas, or concepts, past and future. It is at this very moment where you may start to experience the light of inner awareness, where a feeling of emptiness and all-pervasiveness starts to occur simultaneously. Your still mind naturally drops into the blissful radiance of the heart and, as time becomes timeless, you are *The One*. You are experiencing the opening of the middle path, the path of balancing the two polarities of life, the union of Heaven and Earth within man, and the blooming of the golden flower.

The nice thing about emptiness is that your mind is permitted to experience the dissolving sensations of the outer illusion generated by the self and others. It is a sensation of vast space in between each cell. It is a unique feeling of being the vast, endless blue sky. Please understand that you can live in this world, outside the circle of confusion, without doing anything extreme like hiding yourself in a mountain temple or becoming a hermit. You can become free of the drama that affects others in their daily life by choosing to live consciously and in harmony with all things, not disconnected from them. When living in this state of awareness, you will be able to conserve your energy instead of burning yourself out with the stress of daily life.

I would like you to reflect on the following questions from time to time. This will help you choose, with integrity, the experiences and feelings that will be created by you during your daily life and spiritual awakening. Reflect on these questions as they will help you succeed on your journey, your spiritual homecoming. Does this situation or object in front of me provide greater clarity and comfort on my path? Do the people I associate with support me on my path in a positive or negative manner? Why am I on the path? What are my ultimate goals and purpose in living this life and traveling on this journey? Questions like these, along with self-introspection and an understanding of your own motives, will keep your path free of distractions and obstructions and anything else that is draining you of your precious energy, which is needed for the great work of discovery and mastery of yourself.

**The Physical Body**

To me, the understanding of emptiness in these great times of change is different than it was centuries ago. The philosophy of the past taught the removal or dissolution of emotions. The body was thought of as being a distraction or hindrance to spiritual advancement and awakening. Some traditions did embrace the body but they used the body as a laboratory of experimentation with arts such as internal or external alchemy. In days of old, many alchemists died trying to create the *elixir of immortality* by ingesting extraneous substances such as mercury.

The human body is more than just a dead piece of wood that houses the soul or spirit. The body is what graciously provides the opportunity for our journey, our realization of the divine. We should embrace the body in the correct way, for without the physical essence, created by the mind, awakening would be impossible. Awakening can occur within us, regardless of the external environment. It is just a matter of time before we actually become spiritually mature through various experiences and levels of the mind while in physical embodiment. In these present times, we must embrace and refine the emotions and blissful energies of the body. This is the essence of who we are at this moment, and it is the emotions that give us such unique qualities and individuality.

We are all well aware that taking care of the body is essential for healthy, productive daily living. However, it is especially important for those of us engaged in energy work and spiritual practices. Just as with the athlete, anyone engaging in these types of practices must consider diet and nutrition as a fundamental and important concern. To put it simply, if we put junk food into our bodies, the body will use whatever it can get, pure or impure, to convert the calories into the energy it needs to maintain itself. The old proverb you are what you eat holds much wisdom and truth. And what you eat and how much you eat really does affect the quantity and quality of usable energy used in daily spiritual living. So if you are seeking to master yourself and awaken while still in this human body, please eat healthy, *living* food in smaller portions. Fresh dark greens and organic, non-GMO vegetables, live foods and clean water, will make you feel physically and spiritually light. We will talk more about diet and conscious eating.

Living in a healthy environment near green healthy trees is

also very important. Trees are natural filters that free us from the unhealthy electromagnetic pollution and poisonous fogs produced in and around big cities. Trees also provide balancing and are an important source of medicine, both physical and energetic.

## Laughing as a Source of Balancing

In the medical world, laughter is known to be great medicine and a worldwide known method of curing oneself naturally. When you laugh, where does your observing mind go? Have you ever noticed it disappear from you? It retreats into the space in between the spaces until you are finished laughing. Laughter balances the heart, mind, all the organs, and the emotions. Blood pressure is reduced, and stress from daily life is also released through deep laughter. Laughter opens tight blood vessels and energetically allows the physical body and the magnetic body to merge together in harmony. If you want to make the flow of your KUNLUN Energy deeper within the body, laugh when the heart is filled with joy, then you can laugh for the entire world.

If you ever experience times when you feel disconnected from your heart, simply laugh. Try laughing while making the "ha" sound three times. Ha in Hawaiian means *breath of life*. The vibration of this sound will penetrate the constricted heart that has been choked by the resistant mind, which has or is going through some form of negativity. The mind's touch down point, the brain within your head, the so-called mundane mind, is connected to the *jewel of the heart* through an energetic channel called katika, the channel of clarity. When this channel is open and flowing without constriction, the heart and mundane mind are connected in harmony. The mind in the head can now see the light hidden within the heart, in the *Bundle of His*, through the awakened *sky eye*, the pineal gland of the brain or the mystic third eye, as it is also known. The *Bundle of His* is the special place within your heart where your divine essence resides within your body. It is your divine self. The pineal gland has rudimentary retinal cells within it as well as an octahedron-shaped crystal held inside it acting as a lens to see the etheric light of the Way, the downward flow of Heaven. This light comes down through the katika channel and rests within the Ben Ben stone of the energetic heart and the *Bundle of His* in the physical heart. Duplication of the most subtle inner light to the densest outer matter is the phenomenon of natal development from the alchemical unity of the sperm and egg to the full term fetus born onto the Earth from Water. The inner light of the Heavenly Way providing the soul, or Shen, ignites the forty-six chromosomes into cellular division as the starting point of all matter human. The inner light is the mystical breath of life that, following the blueprint of love, creates the architecture of the body and the functioning organ systems and biochemistry that nurtures and repairs it. Ancient wisdom refers to this phenomenon of inner light, and reveals *when the eye is single, the body will be full of light.* In other words, "en-light-en-ment" is the reversing of the process from physical density back to the subtle beginnings of inner light from Heavenly Way. In the Tibetan tradition, they speak of the *drop of consciousness going back into the ocean of wisdom.* All of these concepts reflect the mind's ability to see the light in the heart through the Katika, the channel of clarity, revealing from whence we came and the love that sustains us.

Once you have made the *ha* sound three times, the next

sound to make is *hee,* which you will also make three times while laughing. This will penetrate the light within the heart. After opening the heart even more, the *hee* sound introduces the mundane mind to the awakened mind shining in that special heart space.

For doing Laughter Chi Gung, I recommend you sit in a wooden chair, relax, smile and inhale through the nose gently, arching the back slightly. As you start to laugh using the *ha* and *hee* sounds, bend forward at the waist, towards the knees, to about a forty-five degree angle. Start with the *ha* sound for three repetitions and then make the *hee* sound for three repetitions as well. Now just sit back and smile and let the work balance you naturally.

I suggest doing your internal cultivation when you feel blissful in your heart and clear within your mind. If you are not in this place, try the Laughter Chi Gung any time you feel you need to raise your spirits, especially prior to your KUNLUN Practice. For those who are medicine people, doctors, or healers, try to remember that laughter is the best medicine. No matter how good of a practitioner you are, if your patient's mind is not open and willing to change, whatever medicine you provide might not work. Connecting and harmonizing body, mind, and spirit through the element of laughter after treating them will make your work stronger and your patient happier. Try it sometime.

**Smiling as a Source of Balancing**

I cannot say enough about the benefit of smiling in everyday life, but especially while practicing the KUNLUN System. When I say to you ten-thousand things rise and fall, what I mean is that your smile has both an internal and external influence on you and those around you. Laughter and smiling are important and something we should focus on. Just for fun, I enjoy going to places to experiment with this smiling concept. Try smiling at a person serving you in a restaurant or airplane to see what reaction you get. It is a great form of communication, and after smiling, laughter comes because they both go hand in hand. Smiling at strangers in a natural way usually has a positive effect on their lives.

Smiling is taught by all Taoist traditions and is a source of great wisdom. Many changes occur physically, psychologically, and emotionally when you smile. For one thing, the tightly calcified sutures of your skull start to slowly separate and open to become similar to the fontanelle of a newborn baby. This opening allows the energy to naturally exchange with the universe inside and out, the microcosm and the macrocosm.

In Tibet, monks and lay people practice the Phowa method of opening the crown. When a person has mastered Phowa, the crown opens, demonstrating that they have succeeded in this method. The lama who taught the student this method would then insert a stalk of kusha grass into the top of the head as a sign of success. This is similar to our opening of the crown, but we attain this through energy practices combined with smiling, laughter, and meditations that focus on the crystal palace. Smiling also lifts the internal organs that have been, over time, pulled down by the force of gravity.

Let me give you an example of this. Let us say your heart is feeling heavy. One cause of this would be that the mind is unhappy. If we reflect on this same concept by not smiling, this action closes the crown and its connection to the energy inside and outside of our body. Now consider when you are angry.

The fire of the mind creates more gravity within our mind and body. Remember your mundane mind, reflected in the brain, is connected with the heart and your emotions.

The mind and brain have a direct effect, positively and negatively, on the physical heart. Anatomically, your heart is encased in the pericardial sack. This sack is where the heart floats in neutral buoyancy. When we are *heavy hearted*, it is because the fires of our emotions shrink this sack surrounding the heart, which in turn gives us that feeling of heaviness. Now if you smile, the fire of the mind can be changed by your will to become like water instead of fire. The simple act of smiling causes the pericardial sack to expand, allowing the heart to float more freely within this sack filled with fluid. You will notice that you feel lighthearted, and as you can see, the mind and the brain and our ability to change the brain's perceptions through changing our mind definitely affects the physical processes of our body.

Inside the physical heart is a delicate, yet powerful structure, a mass of cells called the *Bundle of His*. This is the Holy House (Heaven on Earth) where your Divine Spirit (inner light) rests within your body. It is the place that high-level yogis touch with their minds in order to control the functions of their body. We call this special place in the heart, and its spiritual light, the *indestructible pearl, the pearl of immortality* or *the wish-fulfilling gem*.

When you look through the katika channel that connects the mundane mind in the head with the heart, you will see a blinding light, but this bright light does not hurt your eyes. This intense light is that of your own Divine Spirit. If you have ever had a near death experience or have spoken with someone who has, they would talk about seeing the tunnel of bright light. The katika channel is the tunnel of light they have traveled through. When you experience this channel or have a near death experience, you are not actually going outside yourself but inward, toward your own divine nature, the light that never fades or becomes impure.

As I stated, yogis and Taoists alike have learned to touch these special cells, this sacred place that houses the soul. Many accomplished practitioners of the spiritual arts have developed special gifts or siddhas, such as human hibernation, spirit travel, and choosing one's time of death, by learning to control this point with the mind. When one leaves his or her body, he or she will also lose about five ounces of physical weight. The weight is from the spirit light observed around someone who is living or who has just died.

Countless stories have been told of the master who has passed on, and at the time of transition, those in the master's presence witness the miracle of a very bright, multi-colored light upon his or her death. In most cases, only the hair and nails are left behind, due to the fact that those parts of the body have no nerve endings. This represents mastery of the Gold Dragon Body, Indestructible Diamond Body, or Rainbow Body of Tibet. If you are so inclined, the practices of KUNLUN System are tools that can assist you in attaining Gold Dragon Body for men or Gold Phoenix for women.

# Chapter Six

## *Best Times to Practice and Tips on What and What Not to Do*

What is the meaning of time? To me, time is the experience of being: where we were, where we are in the moment, and where we are yet to go. You can also look at it as past, present, and future, happening in the now.

So we must consider the concept of time in terms of when to practice. Think about this: if it were not for the concept of time, how would your mundane mind or ego see progress and movement on the path of enlightenment? We have an internal need to review our progress with benchmarks that are outside of us; this is normal and very human. Without some form of marker, progression or comparison to now and then, our ego consistently and constantly takes charge, reminding us that our efforts are in vain or that we are wasting our time. Our ego in relation to linear time is a tough taskmaster. Time, as a rule, causes us to grasp or become attached to outcome or reward, but this is not the true reason for practicing. Considerations of time are a practical matter and not a taskmaster.

Everyone has a different reason for wanting to practice this system. For some, it is used as a tool for self-awakening, and for others, it is used to improve or maintain good health. For other individuals, the simple curiosity of the unknown world is what draws them to the art. Perhaps for many, it is for all of these reasons and more. Whatever the attraction or reason for practicing this art, discovering the optimum times for your individual practice will help you to balance yourself and keep in harmony with nature.

For those of us who practice the KUNLUN System, we have this wonder called the human body with specific needs and preferences that we must consider. In order to honor the needs of your body and to discover its preferences with regard to time, I recommend doing the following exercise at the beginning of each of the four seasons. This exercise will help you discover the optimum times for you to practice to receive the best results for your body, based on your focus. As each new season begins, take the opportunity to do the following exercise.

Once per hour over a twenty-four hour period, I want you to observe which of your nostrils is open, and which nostril is closed, keeping track of your findings by charting your results. After the twenty-four hours have past, identify the times on your chart where both nostrils are open. This would be the best time for you to practice. My Tao brother who is a doctor, esoteric teacher, and well-versed practitioner of the KUNLUN System explains:

> Maximum relaxed airflow occurs when both nostrils are open and full, providing optimum airflow. This is very important to your brain since the vibration from the air going through the nostrils provides certain frequencies that resonate through the skull bones. This creates a unique and fundamental frequency, and when combined with the overtones that arise from the air passing through and over these skull bones, it activates certain brain components to respond to their higher functions, particularly, preparing the mind for enlightenment and

Heavenly Way. The reason for this is that the ethmoid bone of the skull vibrates most intently and evenly when the nostrils are equally open due to the maximum amount of airflow going through the conchae or turbinates of the ethmoid bone. This phenomenon is called *Awakening the Celestial Dragon*. It is this awakening that provides a greater opportunity for changes from normal brain function and mundane habits to a superconscious state of being and perceiving. It is called the *Celestial Dragon* due to the activation occurring within the Upper Dantien and air element transformed into super-heated steam or the Over-Unity Breath of the Celestial Forces of nature, that which exists beyond matter and speaks of the quantum potential of all things. The quantum potential of all things must be tickled or invited to come in and play via a frequency or vibration. This vibration can be created by the body naturally using the natural process of breathing, in particular the *One Breath* or circular breathing. The resonance created by the maximum airflow of both nostrils provides the crista galli of the ethmoid bone of the skull an opportunity to vibrate with the highest amplitude. This vibration is transmitted from the crista galli of the ethmoid bone to the portion of the dura mater called the falx cerebri attached along the mid sagital line of the skull, sitting between the two hemispheres of the brain. The vibration transmitted along the falx will provide the same equal and highly energetic vibration to the pineal gland and the fluid-filled ventricles of the brain. The increase in electric charge is due to the piezoelectric effect of those vibrations hitting against the ependymal cells of the ventricles, thus increasing the electrical potential. By increasing the energetic potential of the brain's neural matrix, we are given a greater opportunity to turn on new and never before activated neural wirings within the brain. The newly activated axonal connections add greater potential for free association and unbiased cognition, providing greater opportunity to operate within the realm of the superconscious. The newly formed wiring can now overshadow old repeated patterns that no longer serve us. Simultaneously, as maximum airflow proceeds through the nostrils and into the nasopharynx, the vibrational frequency and strength of those frequencies vibrates the sphenoid sinus inside the sphenoid bone just above the nasopharynx, which vibrates the pituitary gland and prepares it for a greater function beyond its mundane physiological purposes. The pituitary gland, which is *yin* in nature, is prepared to mate with its male or *yang* counterpart, the pineal gland, into Tao coherence or duality brought into perfect balance. As the *Celestial Dragon* awakens, the polar opposite charge of the yin and yang energies most readily merge into pure magnetic potential. It is at this time when the Sushumna channel, as it is called in the Yogic traditions, or the thrusting channel, as it is known in Taoist tradition, is most open, providing the greatest opportunity for an increase in electrical field strength, the production of a coherent magnetic field, and our highest nature to penetrate into the mundane, creating the changes that are necessary for enlightenment. An increase in electromagnetic field strength provides the vital life force the energy needed to create the sought-after changes that occur within the body, the organ systems and the most subtle energy levels in and around the body as well as the micro-components of the DNA. An increase in magnetic potential will directly affect the principal internal brain nuclei that participate in the enlightened mysteries and are a crucial component of the brain-heart connection. The goal with practice is to transcend the mundane and therefore the recognition of linear time in forward progression within our body and physiology. The phenomenon of space-time is an earthly, material component that provides us orientation to the Earth and the Universe in the most mundane and dense aspects of our being. When we create an increase in the magnetic field and then sustain that magnetic field with coherent vectoring, the coherent pattern begins to warp the continuum of space-time and, as a result, time slows down and space becomes open to an adjustment of the gravitational forces, electromagnetic forces, the strong forces and the weak forces to such a degree that with practice, space is now a co-creator with our mind. With clear intent, it is possible to bring density back into light and adjust time to such a degree that its spherical impression on waves of light can allow us to use time in infinite ways, since time is the construct of consciousness. Space becomes filled with the initial gift of love, a tachyon scalar construct, through intention providing light where once there was only potential space and the molecular attraction within that potential space creating matter. This phenomenon is similar to the event horizon that occurs with black holes in our space-time continuum. Black holes have such intense gravitational fields with tube torus-like vectoring that this force even folds light into a vacuum that transcends both time and space beyond mathematical comprehension. Within the vortex of magnetic fluxes, gravity, employing emptiness as an attractor, transcends time and space and goes into Universal Mind. This Mind or reflection of self within the Universe, including our own consciousness and developing density from that consciousness, moves into a point of singularity where infinite possibility exists to create all things. The incomprehensible mathematical possibility where all density including light wave/particle phenomenon becomes one point of probability, but infinite in its possibility, is beyond science and now moves into the mythical transcendence we call God and in its essence can be felt as the Tao. Felt, indeed, for it is the gift that humanity brings to all creation, the ability to feel where mind cannot go and where soul does not tread. It is feeling, created in density by the biochemicals within the limbic system of the brain that provides the direct experience of the brain's transcendence into mind and the mind's transcendence into all possibility. Neither mind nor soul can go there alone. It is the vehicle of the body that provides the mind and soul the opportunity to feel and know eternity and full potential from the void. We were created, and indeed exist, in order to know and feel creation. It is love or the tachyon scalar component that experiences all things without judgment, and thus provides mass to all elemental particles within the quantum potential. The gift of love is the Higgs boson particle that brings potential into the material and allows causality violations to exist going backward and forward in time without the possibility of deconstruction into oblivion. From this point, mind can be freed of gravity, similar to the way the time/space density has been transcended, and Universal Mind is now providing a pure slate of possibility where all things become possible. Soul *lets go* into the ocean of the void, and all things move to Wu Chi and the eighty-one gates of transcendence where Tao is space and Lao Mu becomes time. The number 81 is 3x3x3x3 or Density, Tai Chi and Wu Chi the universal unit of 3 utilizing the (1) weak forces, (2) strong forces, (3) electromagnetic forces, and the (4) gravitational force exponentially, or 3 to the 4th power. The ability to pursue health, longevity, and tranquility are dependent on time through the yearly seasons as well. Every one of the four seasons will have a different expression of the quantum wave component and, subsequently, the scalar effect that each particular wave component creates within the body. Please keep in mind that with every season, the quantum wave influence will undergo changes similar to the affect your own bio-pulses and rhythms have on your behavior and physiology. The changes caused by scalar wave principals of creation, masterfully used by nature to heal and balance our bodies, are powerful and cannot be overlooked. In fact, they are fundamental to everlasting life. The principals of enlightenment are fundamental to nature through the quantum field as the Tao is fundamental to the quantum field itself. It is through nature, the great Taoist teacher, that all things witnessed and experienced can provide the clues that bring us back to source. It is to the delight of our soul that we learn the way of the Tao reflected in eternity through our physical bodies. This is witnessed best with health, longevity, tranquility, and, ultimately, the everlasting body of Gold Dragon or Gold

Phoenix. In addition to seasonal changes, the moon cycle, astrological cycles, hormonal considerations, age, and mental perception all play a crucial role in defining the optimum use of the practice as well as its desired effect on our bodies as we are on the path. There is no need to pre-consider these influences in your practice. This section is written to act as a simple acknowledgement that many aspects of nature do influence the internal alchemical results of your practice, and due to those influences you must be open and without judgment on the effects and outcome of your spiritual endeavors. Each time you do your practice, be open to whatever changes and experiences you have. Do not expect the same results each time. Remember that your practice will be uniquely yours, and eventually the overt movements of body healing will transpose into a calm experience of the emptiness of Heaven, and therefore all things.

It is my hope that this explanation provided by my Tao brother gives you a sense of the power and blessings that nature provides, that which your wonderful human body also holds within it.

Regarding what time of day to practice, I suggest you choose your practice time based on your personal needs and goals of spiritual attainment. You will find a general guideline below, designed to help you learn when to practice for different reasons or outcomes. I suggest making a personal outline and chart as discussed above, indicating what and when to practice.

I recommend practicing once daily at the same time each day so that your body can get accustomed to the meditative exercise and look forward to practicing. Doing this enough times, consistently five times per week, will help your bio-rhythms attune to those specific times of practice. For the first year, do your practice five days per week, taking weekends off so the body can adjust to the new energies. Remember more practice is not better. It is quality, not quantity, that is most important. The only time I would avoid practicing is between the hours of 1pm and 3pm. The reason I say this is because typically after lunch we are at our most intense state. Thoughts during work and negative emotions usually peak at these times when people release a lot of internal negativity due to having to go back to the stresses of work. This is also the time where most people's minds are like fire. So this is not a good time to prac-tice, especially for those who are energetically sensitive, as this time may over stimulate them. So never practice at this time.

5 a.m. to 7 a.m.
Good time for developing yang energy and healing physical ailments.

7:30 p.m. to 9 p.m.
Good time for calming and balancing the
Polarities of yin and yang.

11 p.m. to 1 a.m.
Good time for spiritual endeavors.

1 p.m. to 3p.m.
Never practice during this time

For improving health or for dealing with health-related is-sues, I recommend practicing in the early morning, between the hours of 5 a.m. and 7 a.m. For relaxation and harmonization, practice between the hours of 7:30 p.m. and 9 p.m. This is a time for balancing the tensions between the physical and energetic body. It is a perfect time for this since your mind is calming down from the day of work and stress. This is also the time we have the tendency to just relax and kick back after a long day's work.

The time between 11 p.m. and 1 a.m. is the best time to practice for those seeking spiritual awakening. In our tradition, this time is referred to as the *Hour of Tzu*. This is the time to access the door to spirit that allows us to connect with the higher spiritual masters who assist us in our personal path of awakening.

You may find that you wake up between 2:15 and 3:15am in the morning. This is the time when we are open to receive gifts of spirit, resulting from positive practicing, the hour we receive blessings from the world of spirit. If you cannot sleep during this time, try eating a banana. The fruit will activate your stomach, put the energy flow to rest, and help you fall back to sleep. It is important to know that the stomach is the on-off switch when practicing this art. As we activate the central or thrusting channel through the use of the KUNLUN Method, the stomach turns off.

The alchemical activity of the stomach uses a lot of parasympathetic energy and biochemical focus, causing less energy to be available for healing and higher phases of consciousness. When the stomach is turned off or set into neutral, there is greater opportunity for the parasympathetic component of our autonomic nervous system to increase the magnetic flux field in our bodies. This automatically provides greater opportunity for the central nervous system to create greater amounts of electrostatic charge and for our bodies to hold a greater electrostatic charge, thus increasing our entire electromagnetic potential.

The greater this potential, the greater the ability to harness energy to be focused by our brain and DNA to support healing at all levels, including physical, emotional, and spiritual components of our bodies and consciousness. When we are finished practicing, the stomach turns on again and changes its position, which therefore closes the central channel and returns us back to normal with a better balanced energetic state.

## KUNLUN System: What Not to Do

I must give you a few specific guidelines designed to enhance your practice and to also ensure your well being and safety. This is very important information, so please read carefully.

First, I will discuss what not to do. We have already covered not practicing between the hours of 1 p.m. and 3 p.m. The next thing not to do is to eat or drink one hour before, during, or after any practice. One of the main reasons for doing practice is to create a coherent magnetic field that will, by nature, increase the electrical or qi energy in the body. Once food enters the digestive tract, the accumulated qi will be diverted to the gastrointestinal tract for the alchemical process of digestion. If we wait for an hour to eat or drink, the qi we have generated can be used for creating changes in the body needed for higher states of consciousness, as opposed to being utilized for the mundane mechanism of digestion.

Never take a drink when you are breathing fast or when your heart is beating fast from practicing. Simply wait until your breathing has slowed and your heart rate is at a normal pace. In addition, I suggest drinking room temperature water instead of cold water, which will prevent a shock to your system.

Do not store energy in the head. When you have completed your practice for the day, never, ever, should the accumulated energy stay in your head. The energy must always be stored in the lower dantien, using the special close down method I have taught you.

Do not practice more than once per day. Once daily is enough. Remember quality not quantity is the secret to your own internal illumination. The body needs time to process and must be able to rest and readjust to each level of awakening, so please, take your time and do not overindulge in your practice.

Never practice the KUNLUN Method under the bright sun, as the sun's rays and heat could over stimulate the energy of the body and upper dantien. If you want to practice outside, please do so under a straight and beautiful pine tree and keep your head covered. If the energy becomes very strong and flows to the point where you feel overwhelmed by it, just relax and allow your bare feet to touch the grass. Focus the energy gently to the bottom of the feet, at the bubbling well points, to ground the energy. Never practice in strong winds, as doing so will drain the built-up energies out through the surface of the skin, allowing coldness to enter your lungs.

Never take mind-altering substances such as pot, alcohol, or other drugs while doing this practice. The goal should be to awaken our divinity through a clear mind, not a clouded mind, which sees nothing but its own illusions.

Never practice when you are angry or under the influence of mind-altering substances. The use of drugs and alcohol, combined with a negative state of mind, is a dangerous combination. The KUNLUN Method can amplify your thoughts and ability to manifest whatever is emotionally, mentally, or physically held. This is another important reason why I stress keeping a positive, healthy, and proper mind set while upholding the positive virtues.

As I mentioned in Chapter Four, one of the most important things to avoid is combining the KUNLUN Method and System with any forceful, fire-based practices such as kundalini or any other fire-focused methods. The KUNLUN System, the path of the *water way*, cultivates the internal arts and is designed to facilitate spiritual development. Our KUNLUN Method teaches you how to generate and accumulate energy by using specific time-tested practices that cultivate the downward flow of universal forces. The downward flow of the water path has a different effect on the body and its energies than the fire path practices that cultivate the upward flow of energy. The upward flow of fire originates in the perineum or hui-yin and impar ganglia, representing the flow of Earth upward toward Heaven.

The downward flow of water originates in the heart and cardiac ganglia or plexus and represents the essence of Heavenly Way, the Word, or the Tao. The beauty of man's desire is the ability to merge Heaven and Earth, to bring water and fire together, respectively. The unifying gift of this alchemical interaction is the creation of a *super-heated steam* that, at body temperature, can transmute all impurities of density and sublimate those densities into the light of love and the compassion of the ages simultaneously. It is the *super-heated steam* that provides the superconductive flow of all forces to such a degree that *over unity* to zero point is possible within our bodies, and our consciousness transcends matter to light at the ni-huan and beyond to the emptiness of emptiness or the void.

I suggest that you study the relationship in nature between the fire and water elements, looking at their relationships when in balance and out of balance with each other. We do not want two trains approaching from opposite directions on one set of tracks, so to speak. This vivid image should illustrate what could occur if these two unique systems merge together within one channel of energy. I won't say that the two paths cannot ever be safely practiced, but you need to completely master both systems separately before such things would be possible.

People often ask me if it is okay to practice shamanism with the KUNLUN System. As you may know, Taoism does have some shamanistic roots. With this in mind, if you wish to follow the shamanic path, please keep the shamanic work separated from these energy and spiritual practices by at least forty-eight hours. Do not use the medicines of the shaman with any of the practices taught in this book. If you are seeking such experiences, please remember that this root of connecting with nature has and will always be within you. Your mind and biochemistry can produce the shamanic medicines you need within you. I ask that you simply do the practices and see for yourself what is hidden inside you.

Remember, ninety percent of awakening is in the purification of the mind. Practicing the KUNLUN Method regularly will eventually lead your mind to stillness and emptiness. This level of being reflects the union of body merged with mind without agitation or grasping. When either the outer self or inner self becomes still, the part that is still will calm the other part that is unstill. This occurs naturally when the light from within starts to appear inside your head.

I must stress having NO attachment to any potential manifestation, including seeing the light. Becoming attached to any phenomenon will only hinder you on your path. What is important is that you appreciate without attachment and understand that this light you may see is the light emanation from the divine source within your heart. It is the source within you that starts to emanate brightly as you spiritually mature. This pure light travels up the energy channel that connects the *crystal palace of the brain* to the *wish-fulfilling gem of the heart*. This pathway of clarity, the katika channel, as it called by Tibetan yogis, allows the light to shine upward into the *crystal palace* of the head, where it is seen by the pineal gland. This channel is very important to master and to keep clear of any mental obstruction. I cannot stress enough the significance of gaining mastery over this specific channel.

## KUNLUN System: Important Things to Do

Now that we have covered the guidelines of what not to do, let us continue on with the important reminders of what you will want to do to enhance your practice and spiritual cultivation. At the top of the list are two simple mantras that speak for themselves. The first is "smile, smile, smile" and the other is "ground, ground, ground." You will not only feel better, but you will also have greater success by following and living by these simple statements.

Another significant part of your practice and cultivation is to allow the everyday mind within your head to drop into the special place of the heart. This will shift your observing, thinking, mental state to one of more *feeling*. It is also important to be in the present moment, focusing on the now, not thinking of the outer world, or about the things that you have to do after your practice session. Remember that *living and breathing* your art is the secret to awakening, not just practicing the technique, as you may have done with other arts.

In addition to smiling, grounding, and being in the present moment, perhaps the most important aspect to develop is to combine the mindset of being in the heart with the positive virtues of love, compassion, and joy, which attune your entire being by uniting body, mind, and spirit. Why should we develop these virtues and mental focus during practice? To find the answer to this question, all we must do is turn to nature to reveal the *One Law* found within the essence of the Tao, the Great Mystery that facilitates and supports our self-awakening. The *One Law* is the original frequency that flows through all things, around all objects seen and unseen. It is the living cosmic divine feminine force that animates all things. When we access this *One Law* through the KUNLUN Method and System, our virtuous mind within the secret center of our heart taps into this source of being.

Through our practice, we align ourselves with this frequency, and when it aligns within us properly, the dormant or *junk* DNA starts to awaken because the *One Law* vibration attunes and harmonizes with the DNA strand. The DNA begins to resonate harmonically with this attunement and starts to open and reveal our inner truth. As we continue to practice, this *junk* DNA reveals the natural secrets of spirit, which usually first manifest in the form of good health and siddhas, such as seeing the unseen world and the normal reality through newly developed eyes that Taoists call the yin-yang eye of seeing.

Through the opening of the *sky eye*, we come to understand the hidden truths in this unknown sphere of reality. As we mature and continue our experiences with these realities and understand their purpose, the *sky eye* develops into what is called the *wisdom eye*. Opening and developing the *wisdom eye* allows us to cultivate our gifts at a subtle level in order to help those less fortunate in this life, to help others in both seen and unseen realities.

Please remember that doing the correct things and living your life fully in spirit is extremely important. Live your life the way you wish it to become. To gain mastery, you need to live your life with purpose and integrity to yourself and others in order to accomplish your goals. Do not just think about it, *do it*. Many people talk the talk, but rarely do they walk the walk.

My teachers would always say to me that people in the West often do not get what they wish for on their spiritual path because of their mindset. I was told that in the West, people are busy asking questions instead of practicing the methods as they should. In the western world, we have developed the habit of collecting more and more knowledge and neglect to take the time to practice the teachings. We also fail to master each lesson or neglect to practice what we are given by our teachers who have discovered these truths through their own direct experience.

In the past, my teachers would give me a lesson or practice and then tell me to simplify the practice and master it through my own experience. If I got the right answer from within myself after studying and practicing diligently, my teachers would acknowledge that the outcome of that specific method was correct. However, if I arrived at an incorrect outcome, I was told to go back and practice until the correct experience naturally arose. Part of my training also included studying other traditions to discover and understand the root that all systems have within them.

The path of spiritual awakening is a commitment to one's

self. There should be no if, and, but, or maybe dialogue in your heart or mind. There should be no half way on any spiritual path. Either *you do* or *you do not*. Perhaps it is time to ask yourself the question: have I, or have I not, been following my spiritual path halfway? The solution to any doubt will be found within yourself, clearly marked for you to discover. Keep the path simple, live your life by living your art, trust that you are on the right path for you, be in the heart, live in the moment, let go of attachment, and let go of the need to grasp for something more. Being virtuous in spirit and in deed links you consciously to the divine law flowing within and outside of yourself.

Taoist philosophy states in order to go forward, step back. In order to become full, become empty. This is the doing without doing, the form becoming formless. Another way to look at it is to understand that everything is perfect in its natural state, including you. When you accept this as truth and without judgment, you are able to look at your world and yourself with naked awareness.

Remember the concept of *crazy wisdom*. If you can articulate and verbally describe your experience at the highest level, it is considered the illusionary awakening. The real experience of awakening at its highest level cannot be explained in any form of expression. One who has achieved this level of attainment only laughs about it when trying to explain this realization to another person. Inner truth can only be experienced through the direct internal experience found by practicing arts such as the KUNLUN System or other arts similar in nature.

The process of awakening often begins when we feel that something is missing from our mundane, everyday living. We begin to search, seeking out the truths, becoming more aware, and perhaps wanting to learn more about unexplainable phenomena. Once we find the true root and we start to become awake, we often discover our destiny or life purpose. We begin getting excited about the possibilities of life, the wonder and capability of our human body and our potential for awakening. Eventually we give up the outer search after reading countless books, seeking out multiple teachers, and traveling to the mystical places of the Earth. We come to a point in our spiritual journey when we no longer seek the truth outside of ourselves. With time, a true method of cultivation that is perfect for each of us will be gifted to us by the world of spirit.

We receive this gift directly from the outer, physical world or perhaps the spiritual, inner world. Either way, it is through this gift, this method or practice, that an inner illumination occurs. We may start to realize and believe that we are divine beings. You may even repeat affirmations to yourself such as *I am a divine being* or *I am truly perfect just the way I am*. You would be correct in making these statements, just remember that it is extremely important that along with this illumination, under-standing, and acceptance of our inherent divine nature, that we remain humble. A wise person will walk with his or her head bowed in humility, while graciously accepting and living this truth. After some time of living this way, we realize that service inside is more important than the outer aspects of service. I am reminded of the words of the famous Tibetan yogi, Milarepa, who stated, "When I am alone in the cave awakening myself, I am with everything and everyone."

Your heart is the heart of God that speaks to every living cell in your body. Each of your cells is alive and doing its own thing within your body, but each cell is also a part of a bigger picture, the universe within, the microcosm, and the outer world, or macrocosm. Each cell also represents something in the seen and unseen world, and you and your heart are at the center of that universe. Consider how the universe inside of you has its identical parts in the external universe. To understand both worlds is to understand the deep workings that occur within you and your body. Remember the mantra *Mind is Gravity*. I encourage you to use it as your personal mantra because this statement reveals how your mind affects the world around and within you. With this in mind, let us embrace the path, keeping all extremes of mind, body, and spirit and of all seen and unseen realities in balance. This is what is known as following the middle way or middle path.

Before I close this chapter, I want to make one final recommendation to you, my friend, and that is to never just follow. Never give away your inner power or your authority to another. In Taoist thought, many of my teachers understood and taught that only nature should be in between you and Source. Once you have received a true teaching from a trusted teacher and Spirit has given you the proper method best suited for your path of inner truth and awakening, you should practice with the support of nature itself. This day and age it is very difficult to find a true teaching that will work for everyone. Part of being a human being is to live the journey and to walk the path of the ancients. Traveling here and there in search of masters, getting dismayed with or even being rejected by them and finally giving up the search altogether is a normal expression of self-purification within and for yourself. When you finally surrender the ego self and stop grasping for the truth, the true teachings that are meant for you will finally appear to you. When the truth appears, trust in Spirit because you have proven yourself as one who has asked honestly to be shown a true path back to your knowing, where you will play and practice with a childlike curiosity. You must trust that all you need will be provided to you with ease, without effort or grasping. This is the path of doing without doing. When you open yourself and become self-sustaining from within, the outer universe will follow suit. This is the law of manifestation. Simply let go and practice the arts with a playful, childlike nature and you are sure to succeed.

Now that we have covered some of the commonsense aspects and positive reflections of the KUNLUN System, let us continue this great journey that will lead to the illumination and knowing of who and what you truly are: **Homoluminous,** the human being of living light. This is who and what you truly are. When you look into the mirror every morning, realize that changes are occurring from the inside out and that with every practice, with every moment of *being in* that space of surrender, the great light of awakening will surely shine forth to you, and to all one day.

# Chapter Seven

## *The Gold Flower Method of Maoshan*

The Gold Flower meditation is a simple yet powerful practice that is helpful in opening and purifying the three energy centers called the dantien. It is based on the Taoist *Three Ones* meditation, which incorporates form, color, and sound along with breathing. The three dantien represent the three cavities within the body that store and tune the source energy or Zero Point Energy that the body takes in from the surrounding air. These cavities are the abdominal, thoracic, and cranial cavity.

The first center, located at the abdominal area, is called the lower dantien and represents the bodily level of awareness, the past, and aspects of the earthly plane. Mastery of this dantien is mastery of the physical aspects of one's body and the understanding of the fire element and jing, or essence that is used in internal cultivation.

The second dantien, also known as the middle dantien, is located at the heart level and represents the present and the level of man. This center represents the union of man with the divine mind element, as well as the receptiveness of awakening. The element of water is internalized, unifying with the fire of the lower dantien. When the water of the middle dantien connects with the fire of the lower dantien, a steaming process occurs, which purifies the heart. The middle dantien is the area where jing is converted to qi.

The third or upper dantien is known as the level of heaven. It is the house of the *crystal palace* and the *Hotu* or steps of heaven. The future is represented here in the upper dantien, and as you will see below, the unity of these three dantien takes place here. This energy center also converts the qi into shen or spirit essence.

In review, the lower dantien represents the past, the element of fire, the mundane earth level, as well as yang and the physical body aspects. The middle dantien represents the present moment, the element of water, the level of man, and yin union with yang energy aspects. The upper dantien represents the future, the air element, the heavenly plane, yin, and the spirit level. This is a simplistic approach, even shamanistic in nature. Taoists will look at these balances in their own way, based on what result they are trying to attain. Just remember, nature is the rule to follow.

The dantien are energy centers that have both a color and spin. These elements will make themselves known with time. Based on the physical and spiritual energy level of an individual, the views of these dantien may change over time. Later, as one progresses higher and refines the energy, the dantien will spin faster, changing their spin directions during the inhalations and exhalations.

At some point, the dantien will stop spinning during practice and just emit energy in the form of a directed magnetic field vector and high frequency light potentials emanating from the Tao within you. To activate these energy centers through the Gold Flower practice, we will focus on the sensation connected with a specific hand mudra. The light associated with the three dantien will make itself known to you in time, but we will first need to mentally generate the desired frequency to make it happen.

The Gold Flower Method is a form of internal alchemy. It is the creation of the internal elixir of awakening, which takes the gross matter of the body, the impure elements of the mundane plane of existence and the associated hormones of that plane, and purifies them. When this method is done correctly, the glandular essences are purified and the body becomes more youthful in appearance while the feeling of energy and life becomes more vibrant. We would age much slower if we kept our endocrine glands at their optimum functioning levels. For the higher levels of the endocrine glands to be developed, the lower or mundane level glandulars in the body must first be perfected, especially those related to the kidneys, which themselves must be nurtured like a young infant.

As the third ventricle, also known esoterically as the *crystal palace* of the upper dantien, purifies, the brain starts to create the *Elixir of Immortality* or *Elixir of Life*. In other traditions, this elixir is called ambrosia, the peach of immortality, or soma. Created by the glands of the crystal palace, this ambrosia will have a fruity sweet taste with a thick, honey-like texture. On occasion, it may also have a sweet jasmine or rose scent to it. This nourishing and life-enhancing elixir should be swallowed when it drips from the sphenoid sinus through the upper palate and fills the mouth. When your mouth becomes full of this *fruit of life*, mix it with a gulp of air and combine the two together, then swallow deeply this charged liquid and feel it drop into your lower dantien.

Over time, as you practice, you may notice that the fontanelle at the top of your skull may swell or feel open just like the head of a newborn infant. This experience may also include a drop of thick yellow or reddish fluid coming out the top of the head onto the skin and hair, as this particular fontanelle opening occurs. This opening is a good sign that the glandular union of the pineal and pituitary gland or the yang and yin respectively of the third ventricle and its more esoteric form, the crystal palace, is activating.

In our tradition, we use the purified glandular hormones and neurochemicals brought together in union by cultivation as a source of the alchemical ingredients that awaken the sleeping self. In other traditions, practitioners use shamanic entheogenic elixirs composed of various herbs and minerals. The internal way of alchemy is much more time consuming, but uses the glandular secretions made from various physical components of the human body, such as dimethyltriptamine or DMT made in the pineal gland and lung. Then, through high-level cultivation, such as the KUNLUN System, the alchemical components of such endogenous chemicals are refined.

It is the increase in the coherence of the magnetic field vectors around the body as it becomes superconductive that provides the mundane hormonal component to be alchemically changed into sacred mixtures of active elements that would otherwise be controlled and destroyed prematurely by enzymes, such as monoamineoxidase or MAO that control the half life of these neuropeptides and hormones. Using magnetically enhanced internal alchemy, glandular, organ, and neural secretions created by your own body turn into endogenous sacred elixirs that are more in harmony with nature than entheogenic herbal elixirs.

In our system, we use the breath as a heating element to heat and purify the glandular secretions of the body. The lower dantien becomes the cauldron to prepare our internal elixir of life. I believe it is far safer to use the internal elements of the body than using entheogenic herbs or *outer* alchemy.

## Understanding the Dantien: Their Function and Purpose

In all simplicity and based on the Taoist tradition, the dantien is one of the doors we can use to change the human body into its higher potential. The lower dantien is where the inner fire is awakened through different breathing patterns, which will vary depending on which tradition you are tapping into. In the KUNLUN system, we use the *One Breath* method while others systems use fire-type breathing such as bastrika found in the Indian systems of yoga.

When the breath is combined with the mind in the lower dantien, the fire element finds its proper seat and settles there. Eventually you will feel the root of your qi within this area. When this fire ignites the water element, it will reside in the middle dantien. When this occurs, your heart becomes peaceful and calm, just like the element of water. When the elements are in this order, the rain of the middle dantien flows energetically downward towards the cauldron of fire located within the lower dantien. This is the union of fire and water. When this process of merging continues, there is a steaming process that occurs. The refined energies of this alchemical spiritual union between the lower and middle dantien flow upward towards the upper dantien, and here is where the mind will naturally attain stillness and emptiness, which is reflected as the air element. This is called the place of the *in-between*, a place of insight between the worlds of matter and the void where pure consciousness exists at the *barrier passnot*, the place that summons and yet is seemingly unattainable. Be sure not to fall for the illusionary emptiness. If you find yourself wondering or questioning whether you are truly empty, then you are in the illusionary state of emptiness. To rectify this state of awareness, you must empty yourself of the emptiness.

There are also other manifestations that occur when the lower dantien becomes active. For instance, your body may feel warm and sweaty at times, and you may feel a magnetic coolness throughout your body. When the upper dantien is active, your breath may be faint or soft in sensation. Bright light will be seen from within your head or heart and you may lose body awareness, having feelings of smallness or vastness. Again, these are but a few of the many manifestations that you may experience during and after your practice. Remember, please have no attachment to anything. Just observe, surrender, and let go of any form or grasping at expectations. Most importantly is that after practice you should always store the accumulated energy in the lower dantien. You should never allow the energy to be left or stored in the head. Doing so could lead to physical problems with mental and emotional imbalances that can be difficult to cure.

**Opening the Three Dantien**

Opening the three main dantien is a standard method in most Taoist awakening and martial art practices. When you open the three dantien, you may notice subtle or strong changes in body, mind, and spirit. The length of time it takes to open each energy center is based on the type of method used and also the makeup of the individual in relation to his or her body, mind, and spirit. Some practitioners are more sensitive to energies or more open than others are. Some take a longer time, and others take less time. Some are naturally aware, while others will become aware. It is important for you to understand that it is your determination to succeed and master yourself that is an important factor in training for any art.

When the lower dantien opens and the heat of purification is felt, the body will purify in many ways. Your diet may change; hidden ailments or things unfinished may appear in order to be corrected. Sometimes you may develop aches and pains during joint purification. I know of many people who, being concerned about their cleansing symptoms, have gone to a doctor for professional advice and, after being examined, their doctor found nothing wrong. Any of these symptoms will pass.

When the lower dantien is purified, your physical body will feel light but still rooted into the earth. Remember, the higher the tree grows, the deeper the roots should be. Do not be surprised if your appetite changes or you find yourself eating less volume of food or simply eating lighter foods for a while. I suggest eating six small meals per day instead of three heavy meals. This way of eating will make your body feel and function better without stressing your digestive system from over filling it during your grazing times. You may have cravings for foods that your body has needed but you were unaware of. Foods you do not like to eat or drink may become part of your new diet. These changes are the natural balancing of the biochemistry of your body so that it can find its *middle,* or point of balance. You will notice that your skin will become clearer and more elastic, your flexibility will become better, and, in general, a younger-feeling you will appear.

*You living your practice means you are living the life you have always desired.* Only you can accomplish this. From this point on make it a habit of doing and living your existence with a divine, not mundane, purpose because life's rewards can be great indeed. Again, the dantien will naturally open with time by using a gentle focus and feeling attitude. As you continually practice, the sensation of warmth and heat will become real, and at those times the energy will start to do its work within the body, opening and purifying all the major physical and energetic systems within you.

When the middle dantien opens, a blissful inner awareness awakens within the secret space in the heart. The heart will have a unique sensation of becoming flipped inside out. In the center of your heart exists a mass of cells called the *Bundle of His.* This special place is where your divine essence resides within your body. It is your divine self. Here is an interesting notion to think about: When your heart beats, the energy of this organ always reflects the light of blissful awareness back towards itself. When we open ourselves, the heart starts flipping inside out. This experience allows the hidden light in your heart to shine outwardly into the world. The teaching in presence is realized by you and others when this experience occurs. If you realize the importance of opening your heart through virtuous deed and thought, you will understand that the heart is a prime key to the experience. In this space of inner divine mind, the living essence within your heart is the true and pure consciousness that is you. It is through the gift of spiritual union assisted by the heart that you get to eventually know and unite with the sacred.

Upon death, when it is time to leave your body, there are many portals located throughout the body that can be used for the soul to exit. Your actions and what you did positively or negatively in this life would dictate which of these portals you will use to exit. It is the cultivated awareness of each of these portals, determined by their use and principals of action while in body, that determine the level of realization you would be gifted by the world of Spirit as you leave and enter into the other realms of reality, the outer worlds. The way we perceive our relationship to this world and our conduct here and now will provide the directive for each of these portals in our body to vibrate specifically, opening up the doorway of the next reality we are entitled to visit. It is our passport, in a sense. Based on the credentials held in our passport, Spirit will then use that directive to honor our path, reflected in our mundane world, guiding us safely into the next venue of our reality. Keep in mind that our greatest limitation is the belief system of our perception. I suggest that you study the way children play, how they are in the moment and free of attachment. Or take a look into the eyes of a newborn. You will notice that the baby does not look *at* you but *through* you. Ask yourself, what is the mental and physical state of this baby? If you study this reflection of the baby, it will give you some hints about cultivating your own positive state of awareness and the principals of being without action, without effort, and without control. It is the old adage *do nothing and gain everything*. It is the way of Wu-wei. It is perfect equilibrium and alignment, with the Tao providing a soft and invisible power expressed in the infinite nature of Love, the essence of life itself.

Regarding the heart flipping inside out, imagine, if you will, that your divine essence is kept in place by the beating of the heart. Your heart is generating a magnetic field that acts like an energetic cocoon, so to speak. Keep your heart open and the field will expand. It will become more powerful and coherent. This coherence gives your heart a feeling of lightness and a deep experience of sublime bliss as the coherent magnetic field becomes a tube torus providing a lens that uses scalar energy in a combined explosive-implosive phenomenon of being and non-being simultaneously. Through sound, a phenomenon of sono-lumenessence occurs, turning mechanical vibration into plasma light. Now as you become more awakened through the arts of KUNLUN System, this cocoon becomes more refined, and your heart will become filled with more bliss. This expansion allows your heart to beat in another state of being, one that provides octaves of vibration acting as doorways or portals, summoning the broad manifestations of Divine Love.

As this state occurs either during or after practice, the inner eye defined by the *crystal palace* sees the light hidden within the opened heart. This is the moment of birth, the realization of truth and essence of what and who you truly are. It is the divine union of the mind within the head and the heart merging as one. It is the alchemical production of superheated steam into zero point, under the direction of love and joy, providing you with the awareness that you are all things and nothing simultaneously. The light of our awakened self now shines outwardly from the *Bundle of His* within the opened heart to the outer world. This light is unseen by normal-sighted people but is seen by the awakened. This inner light is the same light that the masters spoke about when they taught in material worldly presence.

As you open your heart and middle dantien, it will fill with blissful awareness, joy, and compassion during your practice until you refine it into emptiness. This emptiness or void can be seen as the so-called vacuum of space. Within the vacuum of space is held seventy-three percent of the mass-energy of the universe. In particle physics and celestial mechanics, as well as physical cosmology, this predominate energy is called dark energy. This dark energy is very powerful. One cubic centimeter of vacuum energy is equal to 10 to the 107$^{th}$ joules/cubic centimeter. This energy, considered to be scalar in nature, gives rise to a repulsive gravitational field, providing the expansive nature of the universe.

As the body and mind become familiar with this playground of dark energy leading to emptiness into the void, the heart will feel calmness during daily life and the body will have a less dense, almost magnetic feeling and unique coolness to it. The heart may feel very large magnetically, as though you are encompassing the universe within it. At other times, the heart, or even your entire self, may feel very small, like the universe sitting on the head of a pin. Remember, *Mind is Gravity.* The increase in the magnetic field gained by practicing the KUNLUN System prepares the body and mind to eventually experience emptiness into the void. Applying quantum theory considerations to the KUNLUN System, my Tao brother explains this very well.

> Given the nature of emptiness, as described above, the gravity attraction effect reverses and now becomes a gravitational repulsive effect, or it can also be perceived as an acceleration expansion phenomenon. As we practice the KUNLUN System, our brain adapts to the physical and neurochemical changes needed to promote the alchemical shift into emptiness, where the mind, which is consciousness one level removed from the brain, is sublimated into the nothing where all things now become possible. This is to say that the attraction or pull of gravity into mass and density or viscosity is transmuted without an intermediate or null phase into an acceleration expansion phase of gravity repulsion that is scalar in na-

ture, tachyon in action, becoming more or less a cosmo-
logical constant that provides the ability to create all
things in goodness and harmony. The possibility of Gold
Dragon/Gold Phoenix Body can now be a reality, offering the clarion call to the Creative Forces of the Universe,
I Am That I Am. Since seventy-three percent of the total
mass energy of the universe is dark energy, this leaves
approximately twenty-seven percent of the mass-energy
to be made-up of matter. On average, the remaining
mass-energy is twenty-three percent dark matter and five
percent ordinary or mundane matter. Now in review, the
amount of brain potential from the whole that human beings normally use is approximately five percent of the
total brain capacity available, and the amount of DNA
that is used to create and operate our human bodies is
approximately five percent of the total number of codons
held within the forty-six chromosomes of each and every
cell. These mass-energy percentages are equal to the way
in which the universe applies its craft to creating the ordinary physical manifestations of supernovas, intergalac-
tic gas, black holes, planets, stars, and galaxies, as well as
the quantum field of particle development and interaction. In addition to the brain and DNA, the overtones of
the heart provide the brain additional coherent energy.
The piezoelectric effect of the heart sounds impact the
ependymal lining of the cerebrospinal-fluid-filled ventricles. The brain uses only about five percent of the total
overtone quality that the heart generates. When the tachyon love energy is maximized through the feeling of
compassion and bliss, the overtone quality of the heart is
made so coherent and abundant that it brings the cortical

neural activity, neuroglial supportive tissue, and deep brain nuclei into harmony, providing a reduction in non-coherent electrical wave forms. The overlying chatter of the unconscious begins to quiet, providing access, in a focused way, to our super-conscious capacity. When this occurs, recognition of the connection to all things and the transmuting power that our thoughts can provide to the quantum field of potential or dark energy begins in a re-newed and powerful way. Gravity no longer directs our full capacity in the world of five percent possibility. Love creates an embedded fractal of accelerated expansion or gravitational repulsion that now determines what is possible within the ninety-five percent of pure potential (dark matter and dark energy). Just as the universe is accelerating into greater and greater expansion and capacity, our super-consciousness now provides us with the unlimited possibility of co-creation with the quantum universe. This means that ninety-five percent of the reality is left for our pleasure to access and acquire, play and create, just as the universe does, providing us with unlimited access to potential energy that will be focused by our intention using the internal lens of our brain, heart, and DNA to create anything we choose. As the KUNLUN System is applied on a regular basis, the increase in coherent magnetism within our bodies accelerates the accessible energy or electrical current dramatically. The vectoring of the coherent magnetic field through intention creates a quasi lenticular lens that amplifies the limitless dark energy neutrino sea into finite body organs such as the kidneys, liver, bone marrow, brain, heart, DNA, and blood. This provides the possibility for an alchemical shift of the DNA and the brain into a superconductive nature at body temperature (98.5° F). When superconductivity occurs, the coherent magnetic field that once penetrated and opened up our bodies to generate large amounts of unusual and non-sustainable energy pushes away from the internal structures of the body and now dances on the outside of our body's shape. The increase in magnetic flux is conserved but is now located outside the conductor, our bodies, not deep inside any longer. This is called the Meissner effect. In addition, the resistance to electrical flow defined by Ohm's Law, $R=V/I$, goes to zero in a superconductive state since the dynamic driving force or voltage (V) of amperage (I) or electron flow against resistance (R) in normal Newtonian physics now goes to zero and the energy in the body is now sustained indefinitely as light. In practice, electrical current will flow through a wire that has gone superconductive at the right critical temperature, usually at low Kelvin, for over 100,000 years without a driving force such as voltage to make the electrical particles move. This is most likely caused by mundane matter now partnered with the largest mass-energy of the universe, dark energy. When this partnership is created and nurtured with consistent practice using the KUNLUN System, a shift in the body's physical form can occur. The physical matter of the body can sublimate into a quasi-gaseous state of plasma light. This plasma field combined with the surface magnetic flux along with the scalar intention from our brain, heart, and DNA holds the form together as the molecular structure of our bodies now participates in the otherwise elusive unified field. In essence, this is the ancient Taoist wisdom and experience spoken of over 5000 years ago. For the adept, the body now partners with the Tao to create the Gold Dragon/Gold Phoenix Body. It is believed that the electrical energy within the body is transmuted from a particle to a wave, creating primal light in and throughout the body. The non-penetrating magnetic field surrounding the now-luminous body keeps the form intact and allows for a reversal of the gravitational field into acceleration expansion. When superconductivity occurs, the rules that create five percent of what we experience in the mundane reality change. There is now a fluidity of matter that creates many unique possibilities and allows one's natural abilities to manifest. Instead of working with only five percent of the body's manifest mundane identity, the adept has now partnered with the rest of creation, opening up the remaining ninety-five percent of the magic held within the microcosmic flow of our bodies, reflecting outwardly to the universe at large. The statement *as above, so below* now becomes acutely apparent as the adept begins the process of learning the finer details of this new manifest awareness and capability. The light body of unity demonstrated by embedded non-destructive wave forms and the tachyon capability to transcend time and space by moving faster than the speed of light provides access to transformative powers that offer intentional and creative capabilities that are boundless and infinite.

It is my hope that the contribution offered by my Tao brother will bring a level understanding to those seeking a scientific explanation of the otherwise inexplicable phenomena that can occur during and after we practice. You see, when the upper dantien is opened, golden light fills the space of the head. Sometimes it will look as though you are seeing the night sky, but in actuality, your *sky eye* is open and your mundane mind is looking at the neurons firing within your own brain via the pineal gland. Your *sky eye,* being stimulated, experiences light beyond light or light beyond the visible spectrum. As the crystal palace, the upper dantien, opens, you may also notice lilac, rose, and lavender scents. The mundane mind may feel very vast, and it *truly is* when freed of the limitations of the pull of gravity.

You may find that your spirit becomes quiet and mysterious, revealing drops of truth to your developing, accelerating, expanding mind. To me, this experience signifies the drop of the awakening mind going into the vast ocean of wisdom. At this level of personal experience, laughter will usually occur as one understands the light of Tao from the level of immersing oneself into the fullness of this experience. I believe that the experience of *crazy wisdom,* as the Tibetan yogis refer to it, relates directly to the endless joy of being in this space of unlimited potential.

When the three dantien are open, there is a humble, egoless being that arises from the ashes of the lower mind, much as a newly born phoenix arising from the ashes, changing from its *old* self into its reborn *new* self. When doing the Gold Flower practice, simply hold the hand mudra and keep the proper focus. Experience the heat generating at the lower dantien, the coolness of the middle dantien, and the emptiness of the upper dantien. This is the simplest way to awaken and purify these centers.

You may discover that other practices regarding the Gold Flower do exist, including a form called reversing the microcosmic flow of the golden flower. This is an entirely different approach and will not be covered in this book.

## Hand Mudra of the Golden Flower

The particular Maoshan method of the Gold Flower that I learned and share with you awakens and purifies the three dantien. This method teaches that qi is represented by the metal element, reflected in the middle finger. You may find that other systems have different approaches, interpretations, and meanings with regard to hand mudras and postures. I cannot comment on what other traditions say or do, I can only speak about the mudras and practices that I have learned and now teach to you. This middle finger will make the connection with the earth element, represented by your thumb. The fingertips should touch lightly together, never with strength because the finger tension would block the flow of energy through the fingers. As you see in the illustration, the hands will touch each other in this practice, with each middle finger touching the tip of each thumb. Try taking one of your hands in the mudra and place it against a mirror. Note the reflection of your hand and the image in the mirror; this is how both hands should look when they are placed together. Now sit on the edge of your chair with your feet flat and spine and neck comfortably straight; open the eyes half way and rest your tongue at the upper palate.

Make a light smile and drop your thoughts into your heart, keeping a childlike nature. Place each hand in the proper mudra so they face each other and touch on the centerline of your body. Drop your united hands in front of your lower dantien and see the thumb and middle finger of your left hand connected to the thumb and middle finger of your right hand. You should have thumb touching thumb, middle finger touching middle finger, and with the other fingers gently straightened, it forms a rudimentary circle shape or portal. Now touch forefinger tip to forefinger tip, then with the ring finger and little fingers slide them together. Look at the two portals you first formed. Now, touch the back of the middle fingers together. You now have two portals that reflect the two mundane eyes, and the two middle fingers touching reflect the components of the third eye and the crystal palace. If you look at your finished hand mudra, it will look like a capstone from the top of a pyramid (hint).

**Hand Mudra for Gold Flower Method**

Lastly, keep the back of the hand straight with the forearm. There you have it, the hand mudra of the Gold Flower. You can easily see the capstone and pyramid shape if you are in proper alignment. Your physical body is now prepared with the proper key, and we are ready to step forth on the path of the Gold Flower.

## Bringing the Three Flowers to the Top

There are two ways of doing this method. The traditional way is to hold the mudra and posture while focusing on each individual dantien. With this method, you focus on the sensation of energy generated by the meditative mind upon the chosen dantien, combined with the hand mudra. This way allows the minimal use of the mundane mind to achieve results.

For this method, you should be sitting on a chair with your legs shoulder-width apart, feet flat on the ground. With subdued lighting and a peaceful, quiet environment, center yourself and achieve a quiet, peaceful state with yourself. This is the basic preparation for your practice. You can do 12, 24, or 36 counts of respirations per dantien, and you should be utilizing the *One Breath* method.

When working with the lower dantien, allow the neck and spine to be comfortably straight with the eyes half closed. Keep a slight smile to open the crown and let the tongue touch naturally behind the upper teeth. While focusing gently on the lower dantien, your eyes should be looking downward at a forty-five degree angle and focused in the direction of the forefingers. Your hands should be off your lap and extended in front of your dantien. Do not lock your elbows. The idea is to use minimal strength to hold this posture.

**Position One
Lower Dantien**

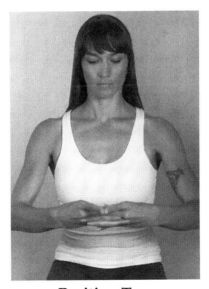

**Position Two
Middle Dantien**

**Position Three
Upper Dantien**

**Three Flowers Rising to the Top**

The next step is to focus gently on generating heat in your lower dantien. Part of your mind is on the breath, the other part is focused on the heart, the eyes gazing softly on the hand mudra. Raise your mudra to the middle dantien and extend your hands forward as you did for the lower Dantien. Look at the forefingers with eyes half closed, and focus on generating a cool spirit. Feel a calm, joyful spirit full of bliss at the level of the middle dantien, with the same number of *One Breath* repetitions you did with the lower dantien.

Now we enter into the third or upper dantien. Keeping the same hand mudra, point the fingers upward to form the capstone shape I discussed earlier. Touch the thumb and middle finger points of your mudra to the point between your eyebrows, the gate of truth. Now your eyes will look upward toward this point in the space between the eyebrows. You will repeat the *One Breath* for the same number of repetitions you did for the other dantien.

After you have worked with each of the three dantien, you will close down by separating your hands and placing them onto your lower dantien, right palm over the left, with the palms facing toward the body. Close your eyes slightly, smile, and allow any and all energy created or felt to sink gently into the lower dantien where the accumulated energy will be stored. I suggest taking a few moments to close down, grounding the energy until your body and mind are calm and peaceful. Please do not eat or drink for at least one hour if you are doing this without guidance so that the energy can stabilize properly in the lower dantien. Eventually the energy will build and equalize within the three dantien. The jing or essence of man will purify and rise to nourish the brain after unifying with the feminine nature held within your heart. It is at this level that the jing essence converts into qi as it reaches the middle dantien. This refined essence continues through the energy pathways, up-ward, toward the third dantien to become shen or spiritual essence. This rising is called the *three flowers blooming and arising* to the top of the head. The blooming of the Gold Flower is when the energy of the three dantien merges one after another togeth-er to finally flow through the aperture of the crown. People with the *sky eye* open would see a beautiful bright golden lotus composed of light flowing from the crown of this practitioner, connecting either with the universe or flowing around the person's magnetic field like a sparkling rain of blissful light.

As you can see, the Gold Flower practice is simple to do and is suitable for the impatient person and for those who need to build the energy slowly and gently.

## The Gold Flower the KUNLUN Method Way

After practicing the Gold Flower method the traditional way for at least a six-month period, and you have through purification developed your KUNLUN Energy, you may now be ready for the next step using the Gold Flower with the KUNLUN Method.

If you are the type of person with little time because of the commitments of life, I suggest this next method utilizing the flowing internal energy and body posture with the Gold Flower mudra. I enjoy this method because it allows one to let go of using too much mind or focus, which can hinder or stop the energy flow at the point of your focus. The internal energy of your developed KUNLUN Energy is changed by the hand mudra, giving it another purpose besides purification. The non-attached mind will change as the internal energy flows without being restricted by the controlling mind. Before you attempt this method, you must have already mastered the basic activation posture of the KUNLUN Method, going through the various changes until stillness of self is attained. You should have been practicing the basic postures of the Gold Flower consistently and the KUNLUN Method for at least six months before starting this second version of the Gold Flower method.

When you are ready, take the KUNLUN Method sitting posture, paying attention to the basic posture requirements and alignments. In this variation, we do not focus on each dantien, we just keep smiling while looking gently at the forefingers, allowing the internal energy to naturally arise. The hand mudra begins at the lower dantien. The consciousness of the divine energy of the KUNLUN Method will merge with the hands because of our gentle focus on the forefingers. Your hands will move on their own accord, so it is wise to keep the fingers touching because if the hands separate you will break the flow of energy. Remember NOT to force movement or energy in any way or form. Eventually, the three dantien will connect from the bottom up and your hands will start floating towards the crown by themselves. When this happens you may feel the energy building up at the crown. Just extend your hand mudra above your head, elbows close to your ears, while focusing on your forefingers. This movement will lead to the blooming of the light of the Gold Flower. The posture your body will take will look like the Eiffel tower.

# Chapter Eight

## *The Three Ones Meditation of Maoshan*

T he Three Ones is a fundamental method used by the Maoshan Taoist as a meditative practice to open and stimulate the three primary energy centers: the lower, middle, and upper dantien. This method is good as a standalone meditation and can be used every day in the morning. Just do not mix it with the other practices. If you have the time, I recommend holding the posture for twenty minutes for each dantien. However, if you are pressed for time, you can do 12, 24, or 36 repetitions. The general rule is to hold the posture without becoming over-stimulated, energetically. When you have finished with all three positions, you will close down and store the generated energy by placing your right palm over your left hand at the lower dantien.

The standard posture for the Three Ones practice is sitting on a chair, legs shoulder-width apart, eyes looking over the nose, a slight smile on your face, and the tongue resting naturally behind the upper teeth. If you prefer, you may also sit cross-legged in a yogic posture, just be sure to sit on a pillow so that your hips are slightly higher than your knees, minimizing any stress on your back.

Now that you are comfortable in the basic sitting position, the practice begins at the lower dantien. For the first position hand mudra, allow the thumb and forefinger to touch, and place your hands on your lap, palms up. Smile, opening the crown, and let your mind settle within the quiet space in the heart. For this practice, I suggest you see your inner self as empty, like the clear blue sky. You will place your intent behind the belly button. It may be helpful to know that the location and measurements used to locate the dantien will vary between Taoist traditions. Some teachers say the location of the lower dantien is one and a half inches below the bellybutton; others will say three inches below.

For our practices, I suggest you place your focus *behind* the belly button, the umbilicus. I encourage you to think about and try to understand why this umbilical region is so significant to our connection to source and, subsequently, our emotional well being and spiritual development. Think about how a baby breathes while in utero. Of course! Just as we, as a fetus in the womb of our mother, breathe through the umbilical cord, taking in oxygen and nutrients and eliminating carbon dioxide and waste, so are we connected with the natural source of Tao from Lao Mu into our lower dantien, sustaining us at the highest level of being.

After locating this place behind the belly button, create a white-colored, three-dimensional orb about the size of a half dollar and focus at this spot. The color white represents the purity of your qi within this center. You will now add a sound that will vibrate this center. The sound that corresponds with the first position is pronounced YEOW and is made by the mouth in a gentle, deep, resonating way. When your twenty minutes is up or you are finished with the predetermined number of repetitions, simply inhale, seeing the orb glow brightly, then exhale, letting it dim and gently fade from sight

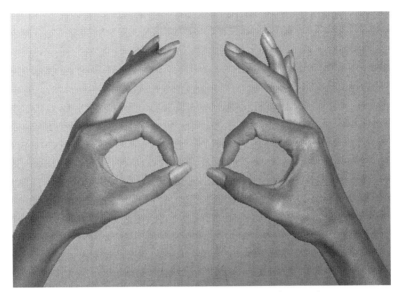

Three Ones Meditation Hand Mudra
First Position, Lower Dantien

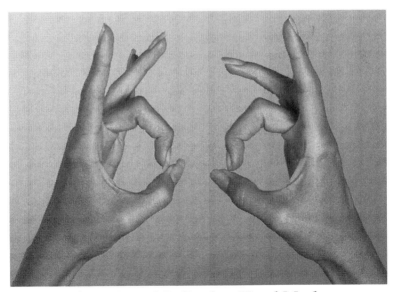

Three Ones Meditation Hand Mudra
Second Position, Middle Dantien

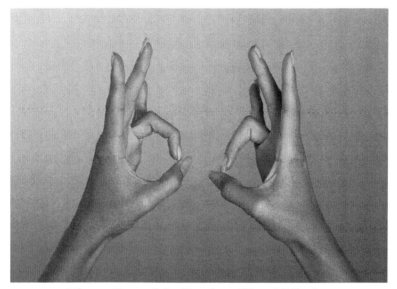

**Three Ones Meditation Hand Mudra**
**Third Position, Upper Dantien**

while exhaling through the nose. You are now ready to move to the second position.

The next position is at the middle dantien, located at the point between the nipple line. For the hand mudra, connect the thumb with the middle fingertip, lightly touching them together and placing on your lap. I would like you to focus in the center of your chest lightly, but not in the heart itself. Remember, in this practice we never visualize this orb in the heart because we do not want energy to congest in the organ tissue. Now create a yellow, three-dimensional orb about the size of a half dollar at this spot. You will see the orb as real and as pure as possible; remember to gently smile. Now with the yellow orb in its proper place, focus lightly on the orb and add the following sound to stimulate its energy. The sound for the second position is SHENNN. Allow the NNN to be pronounced longer than the SHE part of the word. If you create this sound correctly, it will sound and feel like a generator vibrating the body. Do this method for the same time or number of repetitions you did with the first dantien. When you are finished, inhale gently and allow the orb to glow brightly, then slowly exhale through the nose and let the orb gently fade from sight.

The final position is the upper dantien, the point between the eyebrows. This point is called the *ni-huan* or master stem cell. The hand mudra for this last posture connects the thumb to the ring finger and is placed on the lap. To keep the crown energetically open, smile and allow your eyes to slightly look upward, keeping them relaxed and without tension. At the *ni-huan,* the place in-between the eyebrows, create another three-dimensional orb with a violet/purple color. The sound for this position is CHAII-EE. Do not stress the vocal chords when making this sound, as the vibration is more important than the volume of sound. Feeling the vibration and not the volume, and allowing the vibration to merge effortlessly with the light, makes the practice of the Three Ones alive. When you are finished with this dantien, inhale gently and see the orb become bright, then exhale gently and allow the orb to fade from sight.

When you have finished, you will close down and store the generated energy by placing your right palm over your left hand at the lower dantien. With the palms facing the body, simply do the *One Breath* method and allow the generated energy to gently sink and store at this energy center. Remember to smile lightly, opening the crown, and let the energy flow effortlessly down to your lower dantien.

We have now finished the Three Ones meditation. When your three dantien open, you will feel vibrations and perhaps other sensations within these energy centers. Remember to have no attachment to anything that may occur. You will notice that the body, mind, and spirit will change gently through continued practice of this meditation. And with time, you will only get better.

# Chapter Nine

## *Taoist Traveling Hands of Maoshan*

Historically, the Taoist Traveling Hands of Maoshan was used only by the grand masters of our Maoshan branch. This method was secretly concealed in the clan salute, which also represented the branch of our system. The method was used in the old days to travel to the world of spirit, to contact and speak to the celestial masters, whom the Taoist called upon for knowledge, while experiencing the path of Tao. Of course, there have been situations of astral projection or sensations of traveling over great peaks and mountains only to end at some mystical temple to learn from a master now in spirit, and who once practiced the same method.

Traveling Hands can be done sitting or lying down, based on the wishes of the practitioner. Let us begin with the sitting method, but first let me warn you not to do this or any spiritual method when driving a car or operating any form of machinery. The reason I stress this is because the first posture of the Traveling Hands practice looks like you are holding a steering wheel. If you happen to be in the state of mind where your mind is letting go, you could easily activate the traveling just by assuming the hand position.

Sit in a comfortable chair and grab the steering wheel in front of you. Your arms should be shoulder-width apart and bent at the elbows at about a forty-five degree angle. Extend the arms forward so that your elbows are away from your body, slightly ahead of your chest. If your elbows touch your sides, it will shut the energy flow down, so be sure not to touch the sides of the body with your arms. Now open the hands slightly so there is a space between your palms and the fingers just like a loosely held, closed fist. The little finger represents the heart meridian that will open the heart and spirit within your middle dantien. Extending your little finger activates the dormant potential hidden inside you. Allow the tip of your thumbs to touch the middle joint of your forefinger; the pinky fingers should be straight but pointed downward. This is the off position.

With the eyes closed and the arms in the proper position, we will activate the traveling hands by *pointing your pinky fingers downward in a forty-five-degree angle.* Place your intent and focus lightly on the tips of the little finger and allow your mind to fall into the heart, being as open as possible. You should feel a little sleepy, falling into the half-awake and half-asleep state. The traveling hands will only work when you are in between both the seen and unseen worlds. Hold this posture for as long as you desire and simply release the hands when you are finished.

If you are successful with this practice, and are able to do it without anticipating that *something will happen,* there will be a high sound in your left ear. When this occurs, follow the sound back to its origin. You may feel a shaking side to side as the energy body starts to separate from the physical body. You may sense and hear a wind from behind you or you may feel as though you are being pulled out through the spine, or perhaps you will see lines of light in a spider web pattern. These are things you may experience during the separation phase. Your heart may beat fast until you get used to the experience. If your heart continues to beat fast, it will pull you out of the experience.

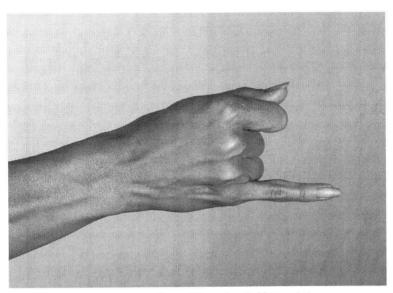

Taoist Traveling Hands Off Position

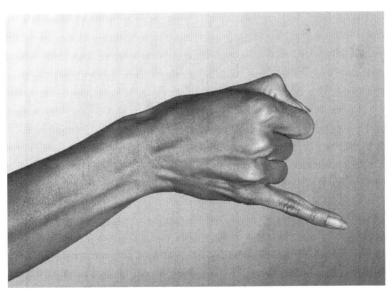

Taoist Traveling Hands On Position

**Spirit Traveling Hands Full Posture, Off Position**

With time, you will get accustomed to the feelings of separation, and the heart will not speed up as you get a feeling for this experience.

As you will later notice, this method is actually very natural and is something that you can do as easily as you can walk down the street. Do you know that it happens to you naturally every night when you go to sleep? Yes, it does, but of course, you are not aware of this process. The Traveling Hands makes it possible for you to notice what has been naturally occurring all of your life, but you were just asleep in your bed unaware of this process. I advise you to have a clear mind when doing these special practices, so do not do this under the influence of drugs or alcohol. I consider sleep time the best time to do the traveling hands, due to the fact that at night, we let the outer world of limitation go and open ourselves to the unlimited potential of the spirit world.

## Variations of the Traveling Hands Practice

There are many methods of dream yoga, each with a different purpose and reason for the practitioner to develop. Let's talk about the sleep version of Traveling Hands. This way of meditation is perfect for those seeking to be aware or lucid in their dream state. It is known that if you can consciously change the elements of your dream, the resulting change has a subtle affect on the physical world. This way we can remove the negative blockages that hold us within our subconscious mind.

When we actually change the contrast within the dream state, the surroundings of the dream change into greater vibrancy, reflecting that a positive transformation of the mental state has occurred. For instance, if within the dream you have situations of running away from something you fear, notice how that thing we fear becomes stronger, more powerful, the more we run away from it. To counter this effect within the dream state, instead of running away from your fear, which makes it stronger, *turn and face it.* Now grab your fear within your dream and do not let go; it will struggle to get away because you have decided to change this fear into a power. When you do this, your fear will suddenly stop resisting and dissolve into nothingness. This nothingness occurs as two individual aspects merge, unite, and create a third aspect. It is much like the elements of fire and water when brought together. When the two opposing elements come together, there is an initial resistance of opposing forces. But think about it for one moment. What happens when fire and water finally merge together? After the moment of sudden contact, the merging of the two opposites creates steam. A harmony between the two opposing forces of fire and water occurs; when these two elements come together and bond constructively, the element of life or qi is created. Once the fear is understood and vanquished, it usually does not reoccur if this process is done consciously within the lucid dream state. Now with this understanding and putting the mind at ease, I will discuss the sleeping method of the traveling hands.

I believe the best time to do this practice is between 11 p.m. and 1 a.m. This is called the *Hour of Tzu.* Lay on your bed using pillows to elevate the upper body at about a forty-five to fifty-five degree angle. Now cross your feet one over the other. It does not matter which foot is over which foot. Laying in this fashion makes us a little uncomfortable and makes it more difficult to fall asleep.

With your hands in the traveling hand mudra, place one

hand over the heart or middle dantien and the other on your abdomen over the lower dantien. For men, the left hand is placed at the heart and for the women the right hand is held at the heart. The hands are symbolic of the water element merging with the heart, balancing, and the lower hand or fire element merging with the earth.

Now close your eyes and let go of all thoughts and breathe naturally. Allow yourself to get sleepy. If you get too sleepy, just open your eyes a little bit. The eyes dictate how much awareness or non-awareness your mind state reaches. Find the proper eye position that allows you to be in the optimum awareness state. Scientists call this the hypnagogic state.

Now, I will share with you the key to opening the doors to experience. If you are seeking a profound experience, simply focus on the little finger of the hand at the heart level. If you wish to be shown things unknown to you, then focus on the little finger of the hand placed on the lower dantien. If you do not know what you seek or wish to understand, merely focus on both little fingers at the same time and let your higher mind decide for you.

If you are seeking to have the astral projection type of experience, focus half your mind on the pinky of your lower dantien, and just surrender. When you feel the body relaxing, let the focus go from the fingers and direct it to a point on the ceiling. As the feeling of side-to-side shaking starts to occur, keep your focus on a point far away from the body. That is it! This experience is what we call the little death. This state occurs every night you sleep, but you are unaware of this process. When you end up in the dream world every night how did you get there? This method leads you to the true reality of the unseen worlds through the use of this key. Later, you will understand through direct experience that this reality, the everyday life, is the dream. Many dream yogis exchange in some form or another this reality with the unseen world and exchange those elements with this world; the unlimited potential of the unseen into the limited potential of the seen.

What typically occurs as you work with this method is that as you fall asleep, the body starts to relax. Then, a creeping cold energy starting from the extremities works itself towards your core, and this sensation gradually works its way upward to the trunk of your body. The next level may include a loss of body awareness, and the heart beats faster because you are not accustomed to the reality of the moment. You may find that as your eyesight and vision dims, an inner light starts to appear.

Your hearing may become very acute with a high-pitched sound heard within your left ear. When you hear this sound, try following the sound back to its source. When you are traveling on this path of sound, you will start to sense a side-to-side movement or a tremor within the body. This sensation is the energy body separating or attempting to slide out of the physical body. In most cases, your mundane mind exits through the head or heart at a forty-five-degree angle, returning through the feet most of the time as you prepare to awaken for another day. As you get used to this shifting sensation, you should focus upward at a forty-five-degree angle toward the direction of the feet, to facilitate the energy body/physical body separation. Remember, the further you focus away from the physical body, the easier it will become for you to perfect this skill. Also remember that this experience happens naturally every night as you fall to sleep. You are just not aware of this experience. This experience is also the same journey when our spirit leaves the body at the moment of death.

Speaking of death, I consider it a sort of graduation in a person's life. Many traditions such as Hawaiian and other cultures have a celebration in honor of the person who has passed on. They acknowledge the accomplishments of that person and celebrate his or her life experiences. When someone in our life dies, we should not only cry, although this is natural, we should also smile and be happy because we never really lose anyone. Not only that, the person who has passed on has succeeded in the path of learning that they had ordained for themselves prior to incarnating into the body this time.

My teachers often told me that funerals were for the living. I want you to understand that in the Tao, in the great universe, nothing and no one is ever wasted. The person who has passed on continues the journey and continues on with the experience of self-awakening within a different context and reality. Some traditions state that if the spirit has felt incomplete in the journey here on this beautiful earth, that in forty-nine days he or she will come back into this physical world to finish those things that were left incomplete.

I have always considered that living in the physically limited reality was taking a vacation from the world of Spirit. We as human beings come here to the physical plane to understand how great and powerful we as human beings truly are. But to understand and live this truth, we need the perfected body in order to have these beyond-body experiences. As we spiritually mature, we realize that everything we see in the physical world around us we have understood and somewhat mastered, and to what purpose those seen things have taught us. But here we all are in this moment, you and I and others are now here to understand the unseen and unknown mysteries. Ask yourself why you are drawn to spirit and to the unseen magic and mystery of the Tao.

I have now given you the Maoshan Traveling Hands method to help you on your spiritual journey. You have two variations of the method: a daytime method and an evening method that you are free to experiment with every day or night if you wish. Choose your path and enjoy discovering the hidden truths and wonders in and around you. Remember this secret if you ever get stuck, your mantra *Mind is Gravity.*

# Chapter Ten

## *Grounding and Balancing the Energy*

In addition to "smile, smile, smile," one of the most important mantras I give to you is "ground, ground, ground." As with all energy and related spiritual work, one should always do something physical after practice. Movement not only helps to circulate the accumulated energy through the physical body, it also grounds the energy in the here and now. One of my favorite sayings is *the higher the tree grows, the deeper the roots must be.* Many people on the path overlook this important aspect and practice of grounding the energy deeply into the Earth. With stillness there must be a merging with movement, with the outer there must be a merging with the inner. To have grounding means to have balance, and it is here that I speak about the middle path and balance of extremes.

Grounding is also the knowing that true spiritual training and journey of one's self is experienced not by trying to get away from the earth and the limitation of life, but to understand that the concept of being in the heavenly realm is, in fact, being in the here and now. The beginning and the end of your path is in the here and now. All worlds and dimensions exist right where you are sitting at this very moment. Just because you cannot see them does not mean that they do not exist. But in time and with practice, the great mystery and all its unseen wonders will appear in some form for you to understand.

Multitudes of people fear going to Hell or being sent to Hell, which is a widely held tenet in many religious belief systems. What is Hell? It is a place to learn and overcome self-limitation by freeing the mind, allowing us the opportunity to sense and become the divine self while in the physical body. We can accomplish the same thing through simple observation and being close to nature. Realize that your self-imposed lesson in this life is to see through the veil of illusion created by your highest spirit so that the divine can learn about its own divine nature. It is our mind, directed by our highest self, that plays out these polarities by creating mental and physical situations in this reality that provide every human being the opportunity to understand his or her unique beauty and essence. We need the challenge of being in this physical shell to understand from an opposite view just what our original form once was. Let me give you an example of such polarity. People fear death unless they have had a close encounter with the breath of death. This element of our life is unknown to us, or so we think, just because we may not remember what that experience was like or cannot remember our past lives. When you overcome the fear or non-understanding of the death experience through this art of awakening, you will come to understand that through the direct experience, death itself is a high form of mind providing us with a crucial understanding of the mundane limitations of the physical body.

Death itself is unavoidable. Who wants to be in a physical body forever? Yes, the time of death can be chosen as well as the transformational state of being into light that the physical body is capable of going through when that transition time arrives. You can research this subject and read about it, as there are many spiritual masters who can attest to this fact. Remember that your body is merely a reflection of the positive and negative experiences of your mind while here on the physical plane. If you were to focus on your positive attributes, you will develop a long life focus of becoming constructive in virtue and thought. This mindset can really extend our life as long as our virtue remains intact and of service to the universe. The negative virtues have a reverse affect. They will only shorten our life in this world. Look at those around you and see the difference these emotions make on the daily and spiritual lives of each and every human being you observe and feel. In the past, I have taken my students to the shopping mall to observe people so that they could see the effect that different virtues have on various people, including the outer and inner reflections they emanate. With keen observation, it becomes acutely apparent that a virtuous mind is indeed important for a healthy, happy, and long life.

Okay, back to the importance of grounding and the significance of living a simple life. All living things are allotted the same amount of heartbeats in life on earth. I often use the example of the hummingbird and turtle to illustrate two very different ways of living and expending these allotted heartbeats. Man can and usually does follow one of these two paths, first going one way, then the other. The hummingbird is a creature that moves quickly and burns its limited allotment of heartbeats by constantly moving and grasping. By living in this manner, it will soon perish. Ask yourself whether you do the hummingbird dance. Do you come home exhausted, not learning to conserve and extend your life by calming your heart and focusing your breath?

At the other side of this extreme, we have the turtle, a creature that lives for a very long time. Why is this? Well, turtle moves with deliberation, eats lightly, and moves slowly, conserving his life force through slow and gentle breathing. Turtle works *with* breath and energy.

I would say that most human beings live by both extremes. During the daytime, we work without conscious control of the breath, the inner fire arises, and we become like the hummingbird. When we come home exhausted from working all day, we become like the turtle, trying to restore the lost energy through sleep. This constant polarity shift causes sickness at the mind level that penetrates into the energy body, then into physical manifestation. When the heart beats quickly, the mingmen or *gate of life* point between the kidneys slowly shuts down. This *gate of life* is your biological timer, so to speak, and an open mingmen keeps the kidneys energized, so it very important to keep the mingmen point open, which can be done through proper mind and body practices.

In many Taoist temples you would see a statue of a turtle which represents longevity, and a snake upon its back representing the rising life force. The turtle would have star patterns etched on its shell representing the stars and energy of the universe. The symbolic meaning in this example helps us to understand the importance of being grounded as a turtle and following what leads us to live a longer, healthier life. The snake symbolizes the raising of the life-giving qi, which helps us by leading us towards the path of the Tao. This lesson presents us with the challenge of finding the necessary balance in our daily lives, so that we can enjoy and achieve all that we are here to experience and master. With this said, let us consider some fundamental grounding practices, including the Five Element practice of Maoshan.

# Chapter Eleven

## *Maoshan Five Elements*

T he Five Element practices are extremely helpful in strengthening the human body and balancing the five major organs and their corresponding emotional components. Aside from their extraordinary biologic functions, the organs can also be thought of as storage batteries for the brain that are used by the body to operate during the day. During our sleep time, our organs recharge like batteries, preparing for the events of the next day.

As human beings, if we use more of one emotion than another, that corresponding organ would drain first and the others would follow. We know that our state of mind, including how and what we think, also affects our body and our organ systems. And we also know without a doubt that remaining positive in thought leads to the constructive flow of energy usage in the body, while negative thought creates a destructive flow of energy within the body.

Each Taoist system has different versions and varieties of this method, and each has a specific intent and purpose. The standing method I teach you is good for physical strength, martial arts, and grounding energy into the earth. If you are weak or have leg problems and cannot stand, you can sit at the edge of a wooden chair, feet flat on the ground, legs shoulder-width apart, and do the same postures with your arms.

Once you have prepared yourself and have assumed your lower body stance, you will hold the postures in a specific order relative to each of the elements: wood, fire, earth, metal, and water. Standing roots us and grounds us to the earth, and the order is the constructive form of the elements. Each element represents and correlates with emotional, mental, and physical elements within you just as outside of you. We begin with the first element and posture, wood. To wood, we add the second element and posture of fire, which burns the wood, reducing it to ash, which becomes the third element and posture of earth. From earth, metal is attained. The fourth element and posture, metal, is tonified by water, the fifth element and posture. Water is absorbed by earth, and the constructive cycle continues.

Simplicity is an important consideration while doing these postures, so I encourage you to resist being scholarly. The standing postures free the mind of scholarly thought, which holds us back from form becoming formless. With time, the energy of each posture will reveal all that will be needed for you to know based on what is needed to be understood. If you are a scholarly person who wants to know the deeper aspects of the elements and postures, I suggest doing further independent research of the five elements, which for now is beyond the scope of this particular book.

Mornings are the best time to cultivate health and wellbeing, so I recommend doing the postures between 5 a.m. and 7 a.m. when the yang energy is more pure. You will notice that your body will become stronger in every way just by doing the Five Element standing postures. You should never practice when you are feeling negative in nature or virtue, as you will only defeat the purpose of this practice. Make every effort to follow the way of turtle and not the way of the hummingbird when doing the Five Elements. Never do these practices in strong winds or in the heat. Do not expose your head to hot sunlight.

Facing the direction of the sunrise for maximum health benefits is great, but do not look directly into the sun. Regarding breathing, I suggest simply using the *One Breath* method throughout all sets of the postures. For each posture, breathing should be from the nose, not the mouth, tongue resting naturally on the upper palate, a slight smile to open the crown, and eyes gently focusing in the direction or level of the hands. First I will teach you the basic stance.

The basic stance is the foundation upon which you will develop the rest of the practice. This stance remains the same for all five standing postures of the Five Elements method. This standing posture will not only provide a sturdy foundation but will also help develop the lower portion of the body.

Standing with feet shoulder width apart and knees slightly bent, slightly tilt the pelvis, tucking the tailbone underneath lightly to release the curve of the low back. Now gently push your thighs outward, away from center, outward to the sides, away from each other. This is called opening the *kua*, which gives strength and foundation to the lower body. You will feel a slight tension in this area. Remember not to force any posture. There should be no pain or stress on the back or the knees.

One way you can check to see if you are doing the lower body posture correctly is to stand with your back against a wall, bend your knees, and tuck your tailbone underneath you slightly. Now try to slip a palm between the spine of your lower back where the curve is and the wall. If your posture is right, you will not be able to fit your hand into the space. Do not force the posture, especially if you are tight in this area. With time, your body will become more flexible and the tight back will loosen up. If after reading this section of the book, and the foundation stance is still not clear to you, ask someone who has done tai chi standing postures; he or she will be able to help you better understand this stance.

We now have your *kua*, the lower portion of our posture, set. Next, create a light and natural smile to open your crown. Push the chin in slightly towards the neck like a proud horse, feeling the upper neck near the atlas; stretch gently, pushing the top of the crown toward the sky. Now relax. As you do this, you should feel a slight stretch in the back of the neck, the spine, and sacrum. Simultaneously tucking the tailbone and tucking the neck creates a counter pull on the spine, therefore extending the length of the spine.

This action also allows the tension of the spine and the three tricky gates within the spinal structure to open. The tricky gates are the three narrowings within the spinal cord. The first gate is at the mingmen point between the kidneys.

The second gate is located in between the shoulder blades on the spine, and the third, the jade pillow, is at the base of the skull. For those who are tight in these areas, I highly recommend finding a good cranial-sacral practitioner to help you open your spine. If you have had trouble with spinal stiffness or energy movement in the past, the cranial-sacral work will help open and soften those areas. So let us now continue with the standing Five Elements method. Do you have the posture aligned properly? Are you feeling good? Has your mundane mind of the head dropped deeply into your heart?

Let us simply breathe in and out through the nose, using the *One Breath*, where the breath is smooth and there is no break between the inhalation and exhalation. The abdomen, not the chest, moves in this manner of breathing. This method of breathing also prevents energy from being stuck in the middle or upper dantien. Do the *One Breath* until your mind and spirit are settled and feel in balance with the body.

You will hold each posture for the same length of time or same number of repetitions, whatever you decide. I suggest holding for about seven minutes per pose for a good effect. In time, you may want to increase your time, little by little, until approximately twenty minutes is reached. If you do not wish to hold the postures for a certain length of time, try doing 36 repetitions of the *One Breath* for each Five Element posture.

In preparation for the standing set, we first do what is called the I-Jong posture, which centers and prepares us mentally and emotionally for the standing Five Elements. It also provides an opportunity to check and perfect your stance and body mechanics prior to your standing set.

To begin I-Jong, stand with your legs shoulder-width apart and set your *kua*. Bend the knees slightly, but do not extend further than the tip of the toes. Now, gently open your knees slightly outward. Tuck your tailbone, relax your shoulders, but slightly round your back so that your chest feels somewhat neutral. The chin is tucked slightly down and back. Press the top of your head toward the sky. Relax and let your eyes look out past your nose at about a forty-five-degree angle. Let your arms hang naturally at your sides with palms facing toward your legs. The middle fingers of each hand lightly touch the outside of each leg at the thigh region. Bend your elbows slightly outward to the sides but do not lock the elbows. Now relax and breathe gently as you hold this stance.

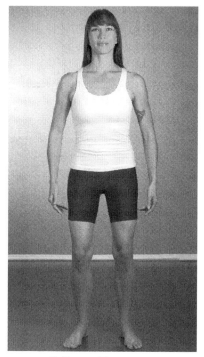

**I-Jong Posture**

**Wood Posture**

The first of the Five Element postures is related to the wood element. You will find that this position increases arm and upper body strength. This posture also strengthens the liver and balances the unbalanced emotions trapped inside of it. I suggest smiling towards the organ to make it lighter, freeing it from the gravity of the mind. Allow your arms to lift from your sides as though you were naturally standing. Lift them to shoulder level, no higher than your shoulders. Sink your shoulders, look ahead with the eyes, smile, and just breathe while focusing on your fingertips. If you are a martial artist, extend the arms with the elbows pointed downward, just below locking the elbow joint. If you are doing this practice for general health, drop your elbows until reaching a forty-five-degree angle. Again, hold this position and all Five Elements positions for the same length of time or repetition count.

The second posture is associated with the fire element, which relates with the essence of your heart. Lift your arms from the wood posture by folding the arms inward towards your center as if you are holding a basketball. Lift your arms upward to about a forty-five-degree angle, your eyes looking in between the backs of the hands, which are close together but not touching. The hands form a triangle shape. Gently keep all the fingers together, except for the pinky finger. Separate the little finger from the other fingers by making a space between the ring finger and the middle finger. Now simply breathe, smile, and focus your mind on the little fingers of both hands. It is important not to lean back at the waist, but slightly round your back, your chest slightly concaved like a dragon body. You should feel balanced with no body stress.

**Fire Posture**

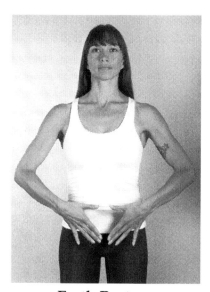

**Earth Posture**

The third posture represents the earth element and is related to the spleen. Earth is especially related to grounding, which is most important in awakening. The hand posture is the same as fire, just lower the hands of fire so that the thumbs face but do not touch each other. The palms face the body, and the thumbs rest in front of the belly button. The other fingers still touch each other, but the thumb is pulled away from the forefinger. When the hands are in the proper position, they form a downward-pointing triangle shape, with the tips of the four fingers pointing towards the earth. The back of the hand should be straight with the forearm, and the hands about an inch away from the body. If your forearm is not aligned with the back of the hand, flex the elbows slightly forward and slightly hollow the chest. The eyes look downward at a forty-five-degree angle. Continue smiling and doing the *One Breath*, holding the position for the same amount of time as the first two postures.

Metal, the fourth posture we hold, is the most important of the five elements. This posture relates to your lungs and qi, the life force within and around you. From the earth posture, raise the hand shoulder-width in front of you until the palms reach shoulder level, no higher. It should look like the pose of superman flying. The palms should be facing the Earth, elbows pointed towards the earth. All of the fingers are gently touching together, your eyes looking straight ahead between the hands. Slightly round your back and concave slightly the chest, pushing the elbows slightly forward until you feel the shoulder blades separate, then relax. Make sure your jaw is not jutting forward. By now, you may feel your legs shaking. This is very natural and, with time, as you get stronger, the movements will disappear. If standing is too much for you, raise your *kua* but never, ever lock your knees; keep the knees healthy and unstrained. This rule

**Metal Posture**

**Water Posture**

applies to all of the postures.

The last posture we hold represents the water element. The water element is related to the kidneys. The kidneys are the most important organs we need to take care of because without kidney energy, balancing is difficult and can create what is called the destructive fire. What do I mean by destructive fire? Water energy cools the body and nourishes it. If the water dissipates, the legs and eyes start to weaken. The heart, usually balanced by the water of the kidneys, cannot be cooled. As the heart begins to beat stronger, the temper flairs and the eyes redden. As fire increases, blood pressure rises, and the lungs pump harder to supply oxygen. The lungs represent the metal element and are affected by the heat of the heart and its fire energy. In a sense, we have fire melting the metal. Now the qi becomes more imbalanced, and we start to become ungrounded, having difficulty in breathing as well as in our daily life and in our relationships. Emotions of negative virtue start arising more often. So as you can see, learning the proper way of energy practice is important. This is just to give you some idea of how one element affects another, and just how important it is to nurture and protect the kidneys.

For the water element, which relates to the kidneys, take your metal element and drop it towards your side naturally. Now turn your wrists so that the palms face forward. Lift the palms to the level of the lower dantien or belly button level. Either level will work. Hollow the palms slightly, fingers touching. With your elbows pointing straight backwards, put your focus gently on the center of your palms, your eyes should be looking downward at a forty-five-degree angle. Smile, breathe, and hold this posture for the same length of time or same number of repetitions as all other postures.

Remember that in all the Five Element postures, the spine and neck should always be comfortable and in alignment, with knees slightly bent. After you have completed the set, you can do the *One Breath* posture with arms hanging down at the side, and then close down by placing your right hand over left, palms facing the body, letting all energy and experiences drop gently to be stored in the first dantien. You can also do something physical, like taking a walk.

So you now have the Maoshan Five Element method. I recommend that you start practicing every other day to see how your body reacts to the practices in this book. Remember that quality of practice is better than quantity. MORE is NOT better. The goal and your success with all of these practices printed in this book is not a question of controlling energy, but rather, surrendering to the cosmic forces of nature lying dormant within you. I highly recommend taking two days off a week to facilitate natural grounding, allowing your body to digest the new levels of energy. Take a vacation from practice and be mundane once in a while. Your body needs time to adjust to the new energies from both inside yourself and from those streaming in from the unseen realities.

# Chapter Twelve

## *Living in Harmony with Nature*

Nature is the very essence, the fundamental principal the great masters drew upon to develop the concepts and ideas that lead to schools of spiritual thought. Observation of nature provided the adept with earthly examples of heavenly way. The *I Ching* or *Book of Changes* tells us that all things on Earth are first an archetype in Heaven. The reason for cultivating qi and living harmoniously in nature is to attain tranquility and to learn of the patterns of Heaven found within every man.

The great masters knew that tranquility could be achieved in all avenues of life by observing the perfect action and the perfect non-action of these natural forces combined into harmony. These forces, defined and cultivated over time, could lead to spiritual realms that, if desired, provide immortality.

The Taoist knew of the importance of sincere tranquility, emulated in nature, in order to enter into the immortal realms and become the ocean of the Tao. Most of us never stop to smell the flowers while on this mystical path. When we walk the path in this way, we miss so much and so many important things. I would like to remind you to remember the small things, for they reveal the secrets of the big things. I believe that the moment that we stepped on the path, we succeeded; our paths complete.

To understand this truth, we just need to be in the proper mindset. This notion of completion is symbolized by the Oroboros, an ancient symbol depicting a completed circle defined by a dragon/snake swallowing its own tail. The entire snake itself represents the earth element. The earth element embraces us, holding our mundane reality in the physical plane. The head of the snake seen as the fire element represents the beginning of our journey, the search for and discovery of our spiritual path. We are tried by fire and the fire gives us the kinetic energy sufficient for our journey. As we move forward on our journey, our walk on the path is symbolized by the snake's body, seen as the metal element or sometimes the wood element. Then, as we reach the end of our journey, we find ourselves at the snake's tail, seen as the water element. The combining of the fundamental four elements along the path alchemically provide the heavenly qi that allows us to transcend our mundane reality. This spiritual energy or qi provides an increase in our life force sufficient to immortalize our bodies into spirit or Shen, one of the three treasures of the Tao.

Now look at where our walk has led us: back to our starting point, the beginning of our path. The symbol of the harmony of opposites is now complete into infinity, united as one, the Tai Chi. The fire and water sublimate into super-heated steam and the heavenly qi, now formed, allows the body and spirit to become one, resonating in the same frequency of light. We, as the adept, are now at the same starting point along the journey, yet at a higher frequency of the reality as we transcend through the eighty-one gates of Wu Chi, moving beyond the speed of light into the void of emptiness. Love, the tachyon particle of possibility beyond light, is what we now become. Our human nature transcends action in the finite to simply being infinite. It is human nature to think that we must move somewhere to get something. If you realize now that the ending point is the same as the beginning point, the symbol of the fire head biting the water tail, our life path takes on an entirely new meaning. This dragon image of the completed circle signifies that the beginning and end of the journey is exactly where you are, in the here and now. It happens in the present, right here, now, in this very moment. There are an infinite number of possibilities along the circle of life as there are along the body of the celestial dragon connecting with itself. Each of those possibilities are available to us, and through our perception that tunes our reality, we either accept or reject those possibilities that eventually determine the outcome of life, our history, and our resonant frequency at any moment. To be in the moment along the path of life as an initiate or adept is the ultimate proof that we have transcended time and space and have become the celestial immortal, the fruit of our quest. If you have any questions about this, just look to nature.

When you are aligned with nature, she reveals to you in some form the solution to the questions. If you wish to understand nature and the five elements, watch how they relate with other elemental forms. By observing the differences of these elements, you will begin to understand and eventually merge these external elements with the inner elements and emotions within your own being. And remember, if you honor and respect nature, it will abundantly reveal the wonders of the Tao to you.

## The Importance of Trees

Trees are a true wonder! They support the planet and us by providing oxygen and shade, they create a beautiful contrast to the moonlit sky, and they sing their song as the wind blows through their rustling leaves. I would like to talk about the importance of trees with regard to general knowing and from a Taoist energy perspective. Have you ever asked yourself what is the most important part of a tree? Whenever I ask this question to my students, some say it is the root, while others would say the leaves.

Truthfully, one part of the tree is not more or less important than another part. Therefore, the correct answer is that the *whole* of the tree is important. It is that simple. When I ask this question to people, those who replied with it is this part or that part used their *thinking* mind to answer. Those attuned to nature, those who *felt* the answer, got it right, and of course, realizing this simple truth, everyone typically breaks out in laughter until I ask my next question: Do you know where the heart of a tree is located? As with all of my students, I give you this question to ponder, and the answer I leave for you to discover.

Different parts of the tree offer various gifts for those who take time to learn. I learned from my teachers that trees were a source of medicine and or nutrition for the mountain-dwelling Taoist. Trees produce various saps that can be used for nutritional and medicinal purposes. For instance, the great pine tree has anti-viral and other medicinal properties, and the sap of the lovely maple tree provides nourishment if consumed. My teachers always stressed the importance of respecting nature spirits and showing respect to the trees, especially when we are receiving some form of energy from them. In my classes, I teach my students how to work with and how to receive the energy and gifts of trees. Let's say we needed the branch of a juniper tree for our health or spiritual needs. Would we walk up to the tree and grab a limb and proceed to break off the branches we wanted without considering what it feels like to the tree? If I came up to you in the same manner and took off your finger, how would you feel? Furthermore, little would be gained from this experience between us. A tree is more than just a vision of beauty or a mere piece of wood to be carved up or used for firewood. A tree is a living being.

When you wish to come to a tree for its healing medicine, select a wide, strong, and straight tree. Introduce yourself and ask for permission to enter its space of life; after all, you wouldn't want someone to just walk into your home uninvited. Would you? Grasp the tree in the *holding the ball* posture of tai chi and do the *One Breath*, softly and peacefully. When you are in the proper surrendering state of being within your heart and mind, a cool, almost magnetic feeling will arise as the tree and your energy become *one*. Once you have made this connection, you can feel and enjoy the energy exchange between you and the tree. Now when you have finished your tree healing and you no longer feel an energy connection with your tree, simply back up and mentally say thank you. I suggest, as an equal exchange of energy, to pour a little water on the base of the tree as a sign of respect. Always come back to the same tree, but remember trees, like people, have uniqueness; some will draw to you, while others will not respond.

When you wish to receive medicine from a tree, it is important to create communication through feeling, and you will find that the tree will be ready and willing to give you its qi, via the sap or blood, as opposed to pulling its energy away, which it will do if you were to carelessly rip or break off the tree branches. As you embrace the tree with the *holding the ball* posture, raise your KUNLUN Energy to the heart and then allow it to flow into the tree until a cool feeling occurs and you and the tree are one. When you properly ask a tree for its medicine, it will allow its living life force to stay in the branch. This way the physical and energetic medicine remains together and the tree gives you the physical and energetic level cure, treating the body, mind, and spirit as one.

After choosing your branch, a simple technique to facilitate this exchange is to hold the branch in one hand, and with the other hand pull the branch away from you. If you are female, you will hold the branch with your left hand and pull the branch with your right hand, the receiving hand. If you are male, it will be the opposite, and you will hold with your right hand and pull away with the left, your receiving hand. You will find you will receive the branch with ease and the tree will generously give you the medicine you seek.

## Understanding the Medicine of Trees

Evergreen trees, such as juniper or pine or any tree that is straight, with its branches pointing downward, gives a cooling affect to you energetically and is excellent for heat-type illnesses. Remember that morning time, between 5 and 7am, is a good time for health and healing because the tree gives off its energy strongly at this time. Trees with branches that point skyward are good to raise internal heat, which is needed to treat cold-related sicknesses. Cedar and some oak trees are good for this type of healing. Trees with branches and leaves that go out in all directions can disperse or balance your qi based on your own level of energy. The four seasons affect the healing potential of trees. For example, during spring, their healing potential is strongest, and during winter, they are weakest.

This chapter is offered as an introduction to the magic of trees. I urge you to find time to spend in nature; observe and find yourself in nature. The Taoist of the mountains has an affinity with nature, for good reason, and you will find that the internal and external methods and practices I share with you relate to the laws of nature. The Taoists are masters at understanding the laws of nature and working with the elements. As you may know, temples are built around the flow of nature. With this in mind, try this little experiment. Do your practice in the house or within a crowded city for two weeks. Take special notice of your body and states of mind. After this two-week period, do the same practices in the purity of nature for an additional two weeks. You will feel a more profound awakening enjoying the assistance of nature. So, my friend, walk the path of Tao, hand in hand with nature, and in particular the great trees. You will find peace, harmony, pleasure, and other great rewards by doing so.

# Chapter Thirteen

## *Importance of Diet*

After practicing the arts, you will notice that at times your cravings, desires, tastes, and even need for food will change. It is typical that depending on what we are going through in life, our eating habits may not always be the best for our bodies. We may at times eat the wrong foods or perhaps over eat. Sometimes over eating is a form of mental protection reflected by the body getting bigger. The extra weight is typically due to some perception or experience that requires the person's mind to protect itself. You might discover that your body craves foods you never previously liked. This is how your body attempts to balance extremes you may have with food.

It is usually not good to eat or drink one hour before or after practice, so as not to disburse the energy into the stomach. I tell my friends who need to eat something before practices because of low blood sugar to eat a banana twenty minutes before practicing. This should help keep you in balance.

You will find that if you are vegetarian and you are doing high-energy practices that you may need more raw protein. What happens is that when you are moving a lot of energy you may need more grounding. Protein provides this grounding. You may also notice that your muscles become leaner. This is due to the body burning the marbled fat that penetrates into the muscle. Depending on how much extra energy the body needs, the yellow fat from within the bone marrow may be used as well. The heat you experience with your practice is from these fats being utilized as fuel.

You will also find that you will be drinking more liquids when doing these practices. This system releases a lot of toxins and crude elements through the blood, so drink good-quality, filtered water that tastes good to you. Glacier ice is an excellent choice. Quality, living water has an inherent vital quality that combines with your body, aiding in its detoxification. If you normally take strong coffee or strong alcohol, consider not drinking these substances. Since we are purifying the body and its glandular system, drinking hard alcohol and strong coffee are counterproductive to our goals. Hard alcohol is especially difficult for women, as the female biology cannot process it. The biochemistry during our practice tries to correct itself, so these things are like putting dirt into clear water. The general rule is that strong liquids over stimulate the body, so find your balance. You do not have to give up anything. What I am offering are considerations and suggestions.

My preference is to drink tea that has been consciously prepared. Tea drinking, which we will cover in the next chapter, is also a very good balancer as well as good medicine.

Many students ask me about taking sacred plants while practicing the art. By doing so, many of you will find that your mind will become clouded with the illusionary light inherent in the plant and its chemistry and not the clear unique light of your own self-awareness. Within your brain, the *crystal palace* can create any and all such sacred medicines by itself in the form of highly specialized neuropeptides. These neural chemicals are then placed into the bloodstream of the body under the direction of the hypothalamus, where they then proceed to every cell in your body. This provides the DNA of the nucleus of each cell the same experience of enlightenment that our brain is creating through the crystal palace. New, never-before-activated codons of DNA within your own living library in each cell of your body are now turned on. These newly activated DNA strands create the modified RNA that determines function and biochemical production of the organelles within the cyto-plasm. The RNA, proceeding from the enlightened nucleus to the rest of the cell, changes the mundane cell structure into the possibility of alchemical transmutation into plasma light within your own body. This process is dynamic and quick, affecting our entire body in just minutes. My suggestion is to practice this art with a childlike nature and a clear heart and mind. You will get deeper and longer-lasting results.

If you are the type of person who has heat-related issues be-cause you are a fiery type person, I would either make your own or go to the health food store and pick up some Ghee, or clarified butter, which tastes great and can be used in your cooking. The Indian yogis use it knowing that it helps insulate the nerves against the building energy current within the body through practice.

Another condition that people ask me about is diabetes. In my Hawaiian tradition studies, I was taught that diabetes reflects too much of one thing. In the Kahuna tradition and understanding, this can be anything. To explore this condition, you would have to look within your mind to see which element there is too much of, or which pattern in your life is in excess.

Most importantly, as long as your body feels clean and fresh and your spirit and heart are clear, your body, mind, and spirit are working together. It is important to treat yourself well; practice well, eat well, and feel well—all of which will help in the purification phase. Remember, living simple is truly better. I tell all my students to treat themselves to something nice each day.

I can tell you from experience that eating light and simple meals, not overloading the stomach with full meals, will make your body operate more efficiently. Try eating six small meals a day instead of three large meals. This will prove much easier on your digestive system. The body is designed to operate without so much bulk food or mass within the stomach, small bowel, and colon.

In addition, you will find that eating foods that are alive, as opposed to foods that are processed or dead, will take up less space in your stomach, decreasing the transit time within the gut. A decrease in transit time while still absorbing nutrients satisfactorily will provide you with a much more harmonious feeling of digestive function and a greater ease in gut feeling. This will provide you with more useable energy coming both from your food and from your own quantum scalar absorption through the kidneys, skin, blood, spleen, and inner glands of the brain. Keep in mind that the food we eat only provides us with approximately sixty percent of the total energy we need to survive and prosper into longevity. The alchemical transmutation of food to useable energy through the bowel and liver is an energy-consuming process and can only be done effectively when we are in a parasympathetic, rest and recovery mode. Eating and trying to digest under stress is counterproductive and forces our digestive system into acid/alkaline dysfunctions and subsequent toxic build up and cadaverine gas production. Eating live foods in small quantities will also help you digest, rest, and sleep better, and insure that you have adequate energy to sustain yourself during practices since the energy needed for alchemical transmutation of food substances is minimized.

As to the amount to eat in one sitting, my teachers would say to open your hand and look at the palm. One third of this space is meant for food, one third of this space is for water, and the last one third is for air. This way of eating follows the constructive law: food is the fire element and drinking water is the water element. Mixing these two together creates energy, just like steam, and the air element moves this combined element throughout the body.

Your body may at times crave something you can't get a handle on. What I mean is that the body will crave living food with spirit, not processed lifeless food. I would suggest for you to eat fresh sashimi, as it is called in Japan. Sashimi, especially salmon, which I eat all the time, will help your body in balancing itself.

Many traditions recommend and include fasting to clear the mind, but I feel that using common sense and not overwhelming the body and keeping the balance between eating and practicing this art will lead you to finding your own balance of the middle path, keeping you away from extremes. I feel that extremes are most detrimental to the body. Remember the saying if the lute string is too tight it will snap and break, if it is too loose, it will not produce a sound, but when properly tightened, not too loose or too tight, the unique beautiful sound may be heard. Everything in our awakening should follow the middle path, the balance between extremes and the space in between polarities. The truth is discovered in between the words, in between heartbeats, in between thoughts. We will find this space when we become balanced through the spiritual practice and great works we are doing.

Remember to use common sense, avoid extremes, and know that you are what you eat. Take joy and pleasure in preparing your food, infusing it with love for your body. Your emotions are directly generated from the foods you consume. Food affects the quality of your mind and inner workings of your body. The function of your organs depends on the quality of energy you receive from your food. All of these factors have a direct impact on your awakening.

# Chapter Fourteen

## *The Art of Tea and Teatime as Meditation*

T ea time is one of my most favorite things to do during the early morning and late evening. Tea is considered a beneficial medicine if prepared properly. Different teas correspond to specific organs and emotions and, as such, I believe that the use of tea is a form of alchemy. For me, teatime is a great time for contemplating life, as it provides the space where time means nothing. I have found that the art of tea allows a spiritual practitioner to become silent and observant of the forces of nature. Gently sipping tea allows the floral essence of the tea to stimulate each portion of the tongue, revealing subtle flavors, which in turn stimulate various mind states within us.

Imagine, if you will, a beautiful morning sunrise, the misty mountains as your background. You are sitting in front of a steaming pot of fragrant, lush, green tea leaves dancing in a porcelain cup. Silently, with steady hands, you pour the steaming ambrosia of joy into a white eggshell teacup for yourself and for an honored guest. You quietly sip this jade elixir, allowing your thoughts to float gently in emptiness, as white billowing clouds float over snowcapped mountains against the vast blue sky. What a great way to practice living the art of emptiness.

There are various forms or arts of tea, such as Taiwanese style, Gakina style, and clay pot style. There are many types of teas, including strong teas and light teas, white, black, red, and green teas.

The immensity of richness and flavors that come from one simple plant is something to ponder. It is fascinating to me that one tea plant creates so many flavors and textures. It reminds me of how, as human beings, we have so many textures and flavors amongst us. So many ways of being, and yet under the appearance of form, skin, and color, we are all a unique reflection of that single tea plant.

When I learned the skills of kung fu tea, I felt I had to share this art with others. As I have done so, I am pleased to say that many people who never experienced this style of tea soon became great fanciers of drinking tea. Imagine the honor a person feels and how special you make that person feel when you offer a simple tea ceremony for them. It brings me great joy to create such experiences for people, many who have told me that no one had ever made them feel that special. Others discover a new simple pleasure stating that they did not know that tea could taste so wonderful.

Understanding the value and importance of tea as meditation and medicine is an important part of Taoist culture. If you think about it, the art of tea is like the spiritual path, and as with any spiritual method, must be carefully selected and refined. The art must be practiced and perfected in order to have the desired positive results. The proper atmosphere of peacefulness, like the balancing of the mind, is most important to truly experience and benefit from the arts. Our spiritual practice is also reflected in the art of tea. In the beginning, tea is just tea, and by experimentation the tea becomes the finest of wine. After this moment, tea is once again just tea.

Tea comes in many strengths, and its quality is determined

by the picking and age of the leaves. The length of time the leaves are steeped gives you many expressions of the tea itself. The elements and implements used in the tea ceremony are very important, just as you have special items you use with your spiritual arts practices. The quality of the water used plays a significant role in the art of tea. The purity of your heart is reflected by the quality of the water.

Some tips for tea drinking include never leaving the tea leaves constantly in hot water. Pour your hot water over the leaves and let sit for a few moments, and then remove the tea leaves from the hot water so the water can evaporate from the leaves. If you leave the tea leaves in the water too long, you will create tannic acid, which is very unhealthy for your body. This awareness of steeping time not only keeps the healthful benefits of the tea intact, it also symbolizes the balance of extremes: not too long, not too short.

I encourage you to learn more about tea, the different types, and their uses and suggest that your training in the Taoist arts include learning the art of the tea ceremony. In addition to the tea ceremony, I also recommend exploring an artistic hobby such as drawing, painting, calligraphy, or poetry. Other choices to consider could be the art of bonsai, gardening, drum making, or playing a musical instrument. Find something to do that is creative and organic, bringing you closer to the elements of life. These are but a few suggestions to help you open yourself to exploring your creativity. We are by nature creative beings, and by engaging in such activities and opening your creative channels, many powerful changes can and will occur. Creative expression will inspire you to appreciate your path and will enhance your experiences on this journey, helping you to express your true spiritual nature. In addition, you will notice how your gift of expression affects others in the way they reflect on their own life. This is what is called teaching in presence, teaching without the need for words. Remember, my friend, there is more to life than being born, growing up, working in a job we don't enjoy, growing old, and dying. Your life is precious. Don't waste it. Find your joy, dream your dreams, and go for them! Make those dreams of yours become a reality.

# Chapter Fifteen

## *The Ultimate Expression of Awakening*

What are the highest manifestations that the great masters before us attained? During my worldwide travels, I have met some of these masters of high attainment from the various ancient traditions. These masters stated to me that in awakening of the self, there are many variations of awakening, just as there are many flower blooms on a plant, growing from one root deep within the Earth. The flower imagery provides an opportunity for comparison of our experiences on this path. Some flowers reflect mastery of the self on the physical level. Other flower blooms represent awakening at the level of the scholarly mind. There are those few who reach the highest possible attainment in which the body, mind, and spirit unite into one total essence while still in the physical body. These individuals tap into the core essence of life, the very root from which all things originate and end. This attainment is known by various names. In the Taoist tradition, it is called the Indestructible Diamond Body or the Body of the Red Phoenix, expressed through the method of the nine palaces, or in our tradition the Gold Dragon Body. In other traditions the highest manifestation is called the body of illumination, moksha or as in Tibet the returnable and non-returnable rainbow body manifestation.

In this state of accomplishment, one can determine how

long he or she wishes to remain on the earthly plane to help those seeking the true path of awakening found within themselves. In this awakened state, you could not tell the difference between this and another person. They look the same as everyone else except in terms of their mannerisms and perhaps their acts of compassion and virtuous way of living. Those who have the *sky eye* open appear as a bright being of living light, brighter than the sun. This bright light means that the person is truly connected with the divine source both inside and outside through the medium of a heart folded inside out. A person at this level may or may not have spiritual powers called siddhas or inner powers. These powers are merely signposts that they are on the correct path. It also means that they carry the true teaching that was passed from one generation of masters to another.

It is also possible for physical manifestations to occur, such as developing large earlobes or marks on the body in specific patterns. Some ancient and modern masters could do miracles for the common people. You must understand that these people are just like you; they too were and are human beings on a spiritual path of self-discovery. So, if they could achieve such things, then so can we, as long as it is for the benefit of those less fortunate and for the good of humanity. These perfected beings had the desire and commitment to do their work to accomplish their spiritual goals. They achieved their goals by following the do or do not example on their spiritual journey. You see, my friend, we will not be successful in achieving our goals if we have an if, and, but, or maybe attitude towards the true path of spirit.

On this perfected or royal path, there is a battle in one's self that arises at one time or another or when we get to a critical turning point on our journey. At times, the ego may come into play and the wanting for power may take over, especially when the non-virtuous mind comes into play. It can happen that we attain something that other spiritual people may not have. There is also the possibility that the temptation of feeling high and mighty, feeling on the top of the mountain, will overcome us. If this occurs and we fall into this abyss, our path will turn sour instead of sweet.

It was told by the masters that many are called and few are chosen. When we attain the gifs of spirit, we should follow the guidelines of the ancients who walked with their heads bowed in humility. We can further help ourselves by avoiding grasping and holding on to anything related to negative virtues or powers.

It is also said that the higher one attains his or her awakening, the less they know. What this means is that you may think you know a lot in the scholarly sense, but when entering into the great mystery of the Tao, we really know nothing except through and by the direct experience of awakening. If someone asks us what is the highest truth and asks for this concept to be explained, we can only laugh the laugh of *crazy wisdom*. I believe that all of humanity, not just the few, has this capability of awakening. It is just dormant, asleep in us. I feel if you live your life as though you have the awakening already, the grasping for awakening will naturally occur less and less and the path itself will become easier, providing greater clarity. If you try to grasp for something in the spirit world, it moves away from you because of your desire. Simply let the grasping go and follow the Taoist concept of doing without doing.

I always say to my friends that the path of awakening is not easy at times. You may find that many of the people around you will not like what you reflect during your process of change. A true master reflects things you may not wish to see. But remember, a master is a being who has overcome his or her own limitations. I have found this to be true, that those who teach the authentic path will cause a ripple through the minds and hearts of others, making them see the unknown. In fact, you may have noticed that masters who taught the true path usually faced great hardships throughout their lives, and many people did not like what they had to teach. Why this occurs is that when a teacher teaches something that really works, many people will not like it because it makes them see the things that they are really hiding from. The master reveals the unknown fears of his or her heart and the lessons hidden within them. This way of teaching has made many a student despise their teacher because they could not understand the concepts of awakening through the direct experience. Once you have identified fear as an emotion that represents something not yet experienced or understood, the fear is no longer there. It simply disappears. Yes, it can be a difficult process but one that is required from time to time.

Some people can be like enemies standing in front of you. In our lives, we meet those who we like and those we do not like. Often times, the people we do not like are those people who reflect things back to us that we do not want to see or experience. As you begin to learn from these interactions between you and these people, they will start reflecting hidden lessons that are waiting to be revealed, held deep within you. As you learn from these experiences, these people will no longer be standing in front of you reflecting what it is you need to learn or perceive. This occurs because you have learned the lessons from the reflective mirror of the other person through the process of recognizing the fear and the introspection of why or how it plagues you. After the lesson is learned, these people may no longer be in your life since you now understand that specific lesson, whatever it may be.

For those of you who teach and have your own students, here is something for you to consider. This story was given to me by one of my early teachers and it has always stood out in my mind. It is a foretelling scenario for one who truly teaches the path of awakening.

When you first begin to teach the new student, that new student will admire, respect, and even adore you because you have put them upon the living path. As your students progress on the path and when the time is right, they will start to open and will have to face their deepest fears and unknown lessons. This is where it gets tricky.

Because they must see their false truths, they will lash out towards you in anger for putting them on the path. As the negative virtues flow within them, they will start blaming the teacher for their own fears and false truths. They may blame the teacher for not pressing the *magic button* to make things better. A true master will make you see your truth, not candy coat your experience or remove it with just a wave of the hands. At this point, either the student separates from the teacher and the teachings or boldly and bravely faces their dark night of the soul. All beings on the true path must, eventually, go through this.

There are some who will resist going through this process, and may get to the point of resenting or even hating their teacher. The student who does not realize that the seeing of one's own fears and unknown issues is part of the process of awakening can get doubly fearful, and in order to cover up that fear or not look at it, they can become very angry. Psychically or emotionally covering something up to avoid its nature is extremely energy consumptive and exhausting. The perpetual fear will often lead to hate in order to be played out if healing the fear is not considered an option in the initiate's mind. Remember, ninety-nine percent of purification is achieved through the clearing of the mind and its energy. The teacher in this reality is the mirror of self-reflection, but the teacher, being filled with compassion, understands this and recognizes right away that this is not a personal issue. After a period of time, the student may come to understand where the root of the anger has come from, finally realizing that it was not the teacher after all, but the self that was responsible for the hard feelings, having this unknowing aspect that was coming up for healing. The teacher was simply the catalyst for the student to see, know, and feel, within themselves, the emotions and closed-off experiences that led to the feelings of fear or hatred exposing the doubt that now provides the healing from the necessary lessons well learned. So, in a nutshell, the lesson from my wise teacher is as follows: "First they like you, then they admire you, then they love you. Later they despise you, even wishing you were dead. Then if you are dead, they miss you, love you even more, realizing later the truth and wishing that they only knew or understood the truth while they still had you in their lives."

Remember, a teacher is only a guide; even teachers do not stay around forever, as they have their own path to finish. If you have ever studied about the lives of the many different masters, you would know that they did not have an easy life teaching. In fact, life was often very difficult for many of them who sacrificed so much of themselves for the benefit of others.

In your search for your own truths, seek the highest possible attainment and masters with integrity that you can find. Remember, there are three primary methods of awakening on your path. The first option is to awaken after the physical death experience, but you have no physical body to experience the fruits of awakening in the physical reality. The second option is to awaken during the death process itself, but your mind is somewhat occupied with the present situation at hand. In my opinion, the best situation for awakening is before the death process occurs. This way you can enjoy the fruits of your labor and also become of service to the universe while still in body. This gives you the opportunity of service while still connected to sensual feeling, physical contact with others, and exploration of the physical world while still being of complete service beyond the physical plane, a complete combination.

With regard to the awakening process, my teachers gave me a simple formula to use as guidance. First, we have to become aware that there is something missing from our reality. This observation leads to our becoming awake and our knowing that there is, indeed, a world of the unseen and the mysterious that can be experienced through mind and body cultivation. Then we have a little death, which is a yogic form of illumination from within, as the heart and the mind merge together through the energy channel known as the katika channel, the channel of clarity, where the mundane mind of the head falls into the blissful radiance of the opened heart. It is here in this place within us where the universe inside and outside meet, the union of seen and unseen, emptiness and bliss melt into One, revealing the true nature of one's own divine spirit.

Please remember that one who is enlightened would never say that he or she is enlightened and that there are many who proclaim themselves as masters. In the past, this title meant something special, not like today. In my view, the title of master should be given to someone who has dedicated him- or herself to achieving spiritual maturity through direct experience and practice of spiritual living. They have lived their art throughout their life, mastering the mysteries of the universe inside and outside themselves. This mastery of self gives the adept the experience of the seen and unseen realities, providing access to the great mystery of Tao. A true master has overcome and changed the lesser virtues and limited self-imposed aspects of him- or herself into the unlimited and newly awakened divine self while still in the physical body. This person has mastered himself or herself and reflects the light of illumination while walking the path humbly, teaching in presence while demonstrating humility and compassion. Also, please remember a true master never forces others to follow his path or claims his path to be the only way. A true master acts as a guide to the complete discovery of one's own inner truth and mastery.

I have never called myself a master. I consider myself to be a simple advisor for the mysteries of the Tao for those seeking my knowledge. When I was much younger, I was given a pearl of wisdom in the form of a metaphor that I have never forgotten and wish to share with you.

*I may think that I have reached the summit of the great mountain of enlightenment, thinking I have reached the very top of Mt. Kunlun, only to finally realize that there is a higher mountain behind the clouds that floated in front of my eyes where I am standing on the summit. I thought I was standing in front of the peak of awakening, but before me in the distance, I see an even greater peak for me to now climb.*

# Chapter Sixteen

## KUNLUN System Final Thoughts

The KUNLUN Method is known to facilitate bodily movements during practice. At times your body may move, and other times no movement occurs. When there is movement in your practice, it means that purification is taking place within body, mind, or spirit. Please remember that awakening is not the movements that are occurring; the physical activations are only purification. It is the stillness and emptiness that brings forth the illumination of self.

Some people who practice the KUNLUN Method start from the state of emptiness and go into movement, while other people go from movement to stillness. Both reactions are equal. One is NOT better or worse than the other. It is common for people to think that they are doing something wrong because they have no movement; they see other practitioners moving during practice, and they are not. Remember, with each day of our daily life we add further experiences onto our patterns or habits through the mental and physical, emotional and spiritual, and also at the energetic level. The practice of KUNLUN System will provide a sustainable method of adding further insight and clarity to our daily lives that will perpetuate higher states of consciousness, action, and being into your life. Just know that each day you practice this unique art, your experiences and revelations will always be different. **Remember this great rule, smile, and have a childlike curiosity and nature.**

Opposite of movement, we have stillness. Cultivating stillness only comes when the mind and body are in a state of non-doing. Stillness is the point when the outer noises and distractions no longer hinder you on your path. It is these distracting noises that keep us from attaining the experience of emptiness. When the outer noises are no longer distracting to us, the inner noises start to make themselves known, and we must quiet our mind even more. These inner noises are the echoes of thoughts from our own lives and the lives of our ancestors and the sound of the heartbeat itself. The more non-grasping we do and the less we seek for answers outside ourselves, the quieter things become.

The quiet can be so profound that we come to a point where we lose ourselves in the ponds of silence. Sometimes in this state of being we may think that we have attained emptiness. This state of being is the experience of illusionary emptiness and results in you seeing and feeling this emptiness through the mundane senses. This state is not the clear light of being. If you empty yourself of the emptiness, the experience of the true light of inner awareness will start to appear. The moment we think or focus on anything outside of ourselves, we lose this glimpse of the emptiness. This is normal. Do not get frustrated by not being able to hold it for long. With experience, it will last for longer periods of time. Another way of reflecting emptiness is through simple observation. When you see an object around you, it has an identity created by you and social consciousness. For instance, you see a tree as a tree, the mountain as a mountain, and so on. You have given these objects power from within you, making the illusion of these mind forms more dense and more real within the constructs of your mind.

Now, I would like you to see everything as a mere image created by your observing mind. Look at these mental constructs without attachment, without labels. What do you think happens when you start to reflect on the world in this fashion? Are you really seeing an object or a form of energy that has been formed by the understanding of what you think that object should look like? The holograms you observe are created by your outwardly looking mind, but as you start to understand that form is emptiness and that emptiness is form, the outer world of illusion weakens its hold upon your mind. The outer picture loses its attractive density on your mind, resulting in you becoming more internally powerful and understanding your outer world and all it contains from within your own universe. The outer world loses its gravity on your mind, allowing you to peek through the veils into the unseen worlds. If you study quantum science, it is said that all things both seen and un-seen are composed of different vibrations of energy. Matter and its density really only exist within the constructs of your mind. Modern scientists and the ancient, awakened teachers taught their pupils that everything is connected within a vast sea of energy and potential with no empty space in between. By understanding this concept, you will realize that all things are light with consciousness, and energy, and light, when slowed down, becomes physical matter. Physical matter is densified pure energy.

Perhaps you have heard about the Tibetan lamas and yogis and other masters of energy who attain the great returnable and non-returnable Rainbow Body, the Red Phoenix Body, the Diamond Body, and Gold Dragon Body. It is described that the person who attains this level of inner awareness glows with the brightness of the sun. When these masters leave this world, there is nothing left of that person's physical body with the exception of the nails, hair, and relics or holy remains. The reason for this is due to fact that the hair and nails have no nerve endings and are therefore not converted into light. The relics, however, are the crystallized material forms of spiritual energy of that person and are considered holy in some traditions. In sciences related to these types of manifestations, it is found that the DNA within our cells has the capability to emit coherent light of one frequency, much like a laser beam in terms of light intensity. The methods of the ancients tap into this concept; after all, the Taoist and the many other masters of various traditions were powerful alchemist and were, in a sense, the early academics of quantum physicists applying their experiences to the world of energy and consciousness.

**Body Movement**

For people who have been practicing and feel they are not having the movement they desire, I suggest the simple refinement of spiraling your body, either clockwise or counterclockwise. When you spiral your body clockwise, energy will be felt moving up the spine. When you revolve your body counterclockwise, your internal energy is descending through the spine. The clockwise movement is the fire element arising while the counterclockwise is the water element descending. I must stress that each tradition is different in their approach to directions and spins. This description is just for the KUNLUN System you are practicing. When purification occurs, the body will move in very specific ways. If your body starts to pulse back and forth your central channel, shushumna or thrusting channel or microcosmic flow is being activated. If your body moves side to side, your sun and moon channels are being activated. Your legs will start to shake, first one leg, then the other. When the legs are bouncing out of sync, this means that the pineal and pituitary glands are not yet harmonized with each other. Usually your legs will come together in harmony, jumping together, much like the sensation of riding a horse. This simultaneous bouncing experience of the legs indicates that the pineal and pituitary are in harmony and the channels of the legs and lower dantien are being activated. The joints may shake loose and crackling type noises will be heard as the energy of the joints start to open, move, and circulate. The joints in your body become reservoirs of energy when all the other channels are full.

So as you can see, the physical movements you experience are related to energy building and circulating, cleansing your body, mind, and spirit, bringing each into union and harmony with each other.

Here is an interesting thought for you to ponder. Do you realize that only a small portion of your spirit is within your body and that you are an extension of everything around you? Have you ever wondered how your mind makes your body move? Imagine that your body is a universe, much like the Milky Way Galaxy. Every part of you within your body has a relationship to some object of that Milky Way Galaxy. Imagine that your spirit, the great light of being, is lodged within your middle dantien. This area would represent the sun within our own solar system and also the heart or center of the Milky Way Galaxy. Physically, this powerful area in our heart is known as the *Bundle of His,* the location where the divine essence, the wish-fulfilling gem, the light that never dims, the messenger that relays cosmic truth, seats itself within your body.

The cells of your body are living within the different structures and organ systems that make up the human body. The basic constituents and components of the cells of the organs, skin, hair, bones, and muscle, etc. would be the same constituents and components of particles and structures found in cosmic space and here on earth. Now, each individual cell would be like a separate conscious being having its own action based on how it perceives its reality. Each cell has an individual consciousness reflective of the larger consciousness held within the collective of cells that in turn is held by the brain, attached to mind. Each of these cells is doing its own part in the world around them while you are also performing and doing what you do as a full human being with the assistance and the consciousness of each cell in your body. At any time, your conscious thoughts can be reflective or influenced by the imperceptible prayers being created by the composite cell structure of your own body. The cells will ask in prayer for harmony when there is none or will demand action when they are out of vibration with the cosmic truth and are operating less than optimally. This may be one reason why you are drawn to the KUNLUN System. The cells' consciousness is praying to you, the larger than life creator, to bring peace and harmony within the environment of the cell or the cell itself. To the cell, this is faith in action, praying to something it cannot see while at the same time knowing that it is part of a much bigger and vital whole. When our mind becomes clear, the imperceptible prayers of these cells are answered by the sun within the human heart. The human heart, feeling every signal of each cell, sensing every prayer request of the collective, provides the necessary input to all vital systems to bring peace and harmony to the area needing it. That input is created in a form of sound that produces local light reflective of the sun within the heart as well as our solar system. The cells become bathed in a unique clear light through sonoluminessence, which provides the ability for the heart sounds to impact onto the cell wall. The cell wall has the piezoelectric components that turn frequency into light.

The sound creates a luminosity of light that is vital to the essence of peace and harmony within the cell itself. These sounds, created by the sound frequencies of the seven muscle layers of the heart, produce overtones of whole notes that stimulate the cell wall and the microtubules of the cell to create light caused by the heart sounds produced due to the request or prayer, if you will, from the cell. It is an ongoing real-time feedback loop.

If the mind is full of chatter forced on it by the imbalanced unconscious thoughts, the heart focus will be principally the brain and what is needed to quiet the unconscious chatter. So much energy and focus is used up by the ego sense to balance our unconscious thoughts. If the mind is clear, the heart can work on all aspects of the body, offering harmony and balance. This unique light produced by the heart sounds miraculously turns disharmony back into harmony within the cell itself and its surroundings. As miraculous as this sounds, it can be perceived by our minds as plausible, due to the research studies done in the quantum field and the theoretical mathematics that suggest how this works, but to the individual cell whose cosmic awareness is limited to its surroundings, this is a big leap of faith. Consequently, to the cells' conscious awareness, the prayers of each cell is answered by you, the creator, through the light created by your heart sounds provided by your own divine nature held within the Sun of Life.

Now to animate your body, the spiritual light created by your highest spiritual essence, which is magnetic in nature, must be converted to a usable form of energy to animate the body. We create the acupuncture meridians that convert the magnetic thought and light impulses into electrical impulse, which then allows the body to move through its shadow element called the nervous system. If you understand esoteric anatomy, the light of the heart travels up the katika channel toward the crystal palace, or upper dantien.

This channel is where the magnetic impulses are converted to electrical impulses, but also where the awakened mind loses its clearness as it travels upward to become the mundane mind. The mastery of the middle and upper dantien and unifying them through this channel is something to study and understand. Again, this description is an esoteric understanding of the process of spirit animating the body, based on the wisdom and insights from various masters I have learned from. So you see, seeking the root understanding of what all systems have in common is very important. Your body is an incredibly unique and powerful vehicle to awaken, not just a piece of flesh and bone. I will tell you as I tell my friends: embrace your uniqueness and never compare yourself to others because there is only *one of you in this entire universe.*

I like to give you things to think about in the pages of this book. I do this to instill or re- instill the mystery of being. We forget who we are in this world. And sometime we forget to ask ourselves, why am I here? Most people do not realize this until it is time for them to leave this world. Some of the things I will say you may or may not agree with, which is fine. I am not here to convert or change your path in any way. I merely wish to share my life experience to those who have searched the world as I have.

Look at this in another way. If you were searching, how much time and money would you need to travel around the world to get to a sacred place, find the right teacher, and then afterwards discover that you did not find the answers to your questions? Indeed, the costs of travel, obtaining visas, hiring translators, food, lodging, and all extras you would need is very high. I want to save you these hardships because the world is anew, fresh, and ready for those who are bold and brave enough.

It is important to live a virtuous life and to have kindness towards others and compassion towards all living things. Also, be kind to yourself. This is a hard concept for some to perfect. Teaching yourself to overcome all obstacles is, at times, difficult. Simply surrender and let go. Embracing your spirit is important.

You, my friend, are perfect in your natural state. You are the alpha and the omega, the beginning and end of the path, which is now in the present. Let me say this in this simple way.

When a great artist makes a painting or when a medicine man makes his sacred pipe, what makes it perfect? Is it the wood, is it the paint, or is it something only directly felt from within? Well, these people, these masters of their art, would intentionally put a mistake, a flaw, into their masterpieces. This *mistake* makes the painting or work of art perfect. So what you see as imperfections within yourself, either in body, mind, or spirit, is what makes you who you are. It is what makes you perfect. You are the perfect artist living within the heart, and the canvas is your mundane mind, so living within the heart and realizing that the flaws you dislike about yourself are what make you the *masterpiece*. You are perfect in your natural state of being.

The great masters or what we call celestial beings will in time come to you to assist you in your growth. These beings will help and assist you using their own experience and knowing.

Many people who practice this unique art will at times see a flashing light towards their left, in the dark. At other times, they may feel a magnetic force around themselves or the presence of a spirit. These manifestations are indications that your thoughts have been heard by the world of spirit. Again, do not be attached to anything. Merely observe with openness this natural state of your being. When you have learned enough from the true teachers of the earth plane, the spiritual and celestial beings will help you towards the next level of awakening. This art will lead you towards your goal without the unnecessary hardships, if you learn to surrender and trust the process. If you live the way of the heart, in harmony and with compassion, while enjoying the simple things in life, your life will seem effortless and really can become the great journey of discovery, with the universe supplying all that you will need.

The following chart provides a few basic guidelines that emphasize the positive virtues that will hone the focus of your mind on the unique qualities within you. Another way of focusing on the positive aspects of your life is to live the virtues of the great masters who had high realizations.

Most people on the path know right from wrong, so use your common sense in practice and hold the teachings of the great masters in your heart and in spirit. Understanding these concepts will connect you to the source of their knowledge. Remember that the great masters were just like you and me.

The KUNLUN System opens the door to potential and possibilities. It is a door, a key towards the great mystery of Tao. It directs you towards the understanding of *crazy wisdom,*as the Tibetan lamas say in their teachings.

Remember there is a fine line between awakening and craziness; it can be like walking on the edge of a sharp sword. Please walk with integrity, balance, and positive virtue. Thank you and be well. Max

| Positive Virtues | Negative Virtues |
| --- | --- |
| Live in harmony with nature and all living beings. | Developing inflated ego and wanting of power. |
| Be humble, kind, and compassionate towards others. | Reflecting negative influences and virtues, practicing solely for financial gain. |
| Live your art truthfully. | Bragging about oneself; disrespecting others. |
| Live your life fully and honestly. | Bringing harm to other living beings. |
| Show respect for others, other arts, and other systems of spirit | Boasting that you are better than others or bragging about your special gifts. |
| Respect your teachers and those who have come before you. | Disrespecting your teachers, the art, and their lineage. |
| Practice with a clear mind, staying in your heart. | Practicing from the mundane mind. |

| | |
|---|---|
| Living joyfully from the heart. | Living with anger, resentment, revenge, or blaming others for your own purification. |
| Honor the body by eating healthy food and drink. Exercise regularly. | Abusing the body with drugs and alcohol. Living a sedentary life. |
| Humbly accept and honor your divine self, accept that you are perfection. | Comparing yourself to others. Judging others, including yourself. |
| Embrace your childlike nature. Take time to play and laugh. Embrace nature and embrace the feminine essence within you. Be like water. | Being aggressive, cruel, or controlling. If you are too fiery a person, be like water. If too much like water, find the ways to balance with fire. |

| **KUNLUN Do** | **KUNLUN Do Not** |
|---|---|
| Set regular practice times five days per week. Take two days off to be in the mundane world. Listen to your body. | Do Not practice between the hours of 1 and 3 p.m. And Do Not overdo the practices. Once a day is enough. |

Drink plenty of fresh water and wholesome foods

Do Not eat or drink an hour before or after your practice.

Explore the seen and unseen mysteries with a clear mind and open heart

Do Not Practice under the influence of drugs or alcohol. You will only find an illusionary awakening

Practice in nature. Just be sure to be in the shade and near trees

Do Not practice in the hot sun, in the wind, or near the ocean or other large bodies of water.

Study the Five elements and their relationship to nature and your body

Do Not mix practices especially the fire path practices with the KUNLUN System

Honor the One Law of nature. Play with the newly discovered energy

Do Not attempt to control nature and the newly discovered energy

Do something nice for yourself at least once per day. Refine your emotions
Explore other arts. Discover creative ways to enhance your spiritual living

Do Not give away your power to anything or anyone. You are always in control
Do Not combine practices from other systems with the KUNLUN System. If in doubt, ask. Or just don't do it.

Embrace and play with the mysteries of Tao.

Do Not get attached to any manifestations or siddhas that you may attain

Smile, Smile, Smile and Ground, Ground, Ground. Cultivate deep roots.

Do Not overindulge in bliss or be ruled by it as it can be addicting like a drug

Relax, surrender, enjoy and FEEL from your heart. Give your mind a rest. Enjoy your life. Find balance, the middle way.

Do Not be ruled by your mind. Do Not grasp for power or be overly occupied with gaining attainments

# Chapter Seventeen

## *History and Science of the KUNLUN System*

To learn more about the history and science of the KUNLUN System, the information can be found on my website, www.PrimordialAlchemist.com. It contains the information on the Kunlun mountain range along with a scientific explanation of this art. The information was written by friends of mine called Brothers Tao. Due to the length of its content and structure, I felt it better to direct you to my site for you to see what is offered in terms of knowledge to those seeking the path of self-fulfillment. May your journey be smooth as you allow your life to bloom, and may you receive all the benefits of the awakening you desire through the use of this path and these arts of internal alchemy. Thank you for your time and efforts in awakening your own divine potential.

If you are called to practice the arts contained within this book, it is recommended that you also seek professional instruction either from the author himself or from a trained and certified apprentice, facilitator, or instructor, as the book offers only the basic foundations of the KUNLUN System.

Remember not to practice while under the influence of drugs, including alcohol or hallucinogens. You are advised not to practice if you have any type of blood cancer, drug or alcohol addiction, bi-polar disorder, or are under the age of eighteen.

# About the Author

Max Christensen, the founder of the KUNLUN System, has studied various esoteric spiritual traditions throughout most of his life. Through his own personal experiences and traveling around the world learning from various masters of awakening, he developed the KUNLUN System.

Max began his early spiritual path at the age of six, learning the Taoist ways of health and alchemy, along with traditional shamanic ways of connecting with nature. Later in life, he was exposed to the Nyingma tradition, Hawaiian Peleku and Kanelu tradition of Kauai, the Native American red willow tradition, Mongolian shamanism, Maoshan Taoism, and the Egyptian School of Tet.

Max continues to teach this simple system of self-awakening through classes and seminars to many students throughout the world, reflecting the positive merits of this unique system.

Max has been on public radio interviews abroad, examined by the scientist of Beijing psychic research institute in China on the positive effects of this unique system, and continues to develop a deeper understanding of the great spiritual traditions through his own personal practice of the KUNLUN System.

*"Remember, you are the beginning and the end of the path that you alone choose. Your own mind dictates how you will awaken, where the path will take you, and what you will attain in this lifetime."*

— Max Christensen

51933543R00115

Made in the USA
San Bernardino, CA
08 August 2017